True to a Type

Vol. 1

Robert Cleland

Alpha Editions

This edition published in 2024

ISBN : 9789362097989

Design and Setting By
Alpha Editions
www.alphaedis.com
Email - info@alphaedis.com

As per information held with us this book is in Public Domain.
This book is a reproduction of an important historical work. Alpha Editions uses the best technology to reproduce historical work in the same manner it was first published to preserve its original nature. Any marks or number seen are left intentionally to preserve its true form.

Contents

VOL. 1	- 1 -
CHAPTER I.	- 3 -
CHAPTER II.	- 9 -
CHAPTER III.	- 15 -
CHAPTER IV.	- 20 -
CHAPTER V.	- 25 -
CHAPTER VI.	- 28 -
CHAPTER VII.	- 35 -
CHAPTER VIII.	- 38 -
CHAPTER IX.	- 44 -
CHAPTER X.	- 49 -
CHAPTER XI.	- 55 -
CHAPTER XII.	- 62 -
CHAPTER XIII.	- 70 -
CHAPTER XIV.	- 76 -
CHAPTER XV.	- 81 -
CHAPTER XVI.	- 87 -
CHAPTER XVII.	- 94 -
CHAPTER XVIII.	- 101 -
CHAPTER XIX.	- 104 -

VOL. 1

CHAPTER I.

PROLOGUE.

It was evening in New Orleans--the brief swift evening of the South, which links, with imperceptible graduation, the sultry glare of day to the cool of night. The narrow old streets were growing dim in the transparent dusk. The torpid houses, sealed up hermetically through all the afternoon to exclude the heated light and air, awoke from their siesta, throwing wide their doors and casements to the breeze. The inhabitants came forth, and sauntered up and down, or sat about their doors, drawing long, deep breaths of the evening air--coming back to life again, and throwing off their languor. It was the hour of rest for the toilers, of refreshment for all, and they were enjoying it in indolent content.

Only one among the many moving to and fro appeared animated by a purpose. He stepped briskly forward, brushing against an idler now and then, but was past before the other's eyes had turned in lazy inquiry to know the reason.

He was young. Twenty-one was his actual age, though he might have passed for some years older. His features and his skin were browned and sharpened by climate and vicissitude; but in his eye at that moment there was no sign of aught but youth and hope and blissful anticipation. Brushing his way swiftly through the sauntering throng, his gaze seemed fixed upon some joy beyond, heedless of nearer objects; and his eyes shone with a clearness like the rift in a moon-obscuring cloud, betraying the brightness and the light within; and a smile was lurking in the corners of his mouth, which waited only for a pretext to break forth in joyous laughter.

Threading his way through the older portion of the town, he arrived at last in the outskirts, where high blank walls overtopped by trees, and houses with their faces turned studiously from the street, preserved the sullen deadness which more populous neighbourhood had cast aside at sundown.

Before a garden door he stopped and knocked--knocked loudly, and with a peculiar tantarabulation, as if it were a well-remembered signal, and stood and waited impatiently. The shuffling of feet could be heard within, and there came whisperings and rustlings, but the door remained fast, and the young man stood and waited, and knocked again, more softly this time, and with a brightening smile as he stood and listened.

"They have gone to call her," he said to himself, "that she may come and open to me herself, as she used to do. Dear girl! It is three long years since last she let me in--three weary years. But why this long delay? She could not expect me, but she knows my knock. Can she be from home? Then why does not some one open?"

Again the footsteps could be heard within. Laggingly they drew near. Heavy unwillingness could be noted in their tread. The young man knocked again. A key turned gratingly in the stiff old lock, and bolts and fastenings creaked and rasped and yielded tardily, as to a hand which trembled while it pressed them. The door swung open, and the youth with arms extended leaped within the threshold; but the figure which admitted him was not the one he had expected; his arms fell by his side--it was not she.

The figure which had opened drew backward with a scream. It was a servant, and in the doubtful light the white-handkerchief about the head stood out against the dusky foliage of the magnolias, and defined the negro face.

"O Lordie, Lordie!" was her trembling exclamation, as she shrank away. She would have run, but her limbs were powerless. She stood staring at the visitor with starting eyes whose whites revealed the round dilated pupils, while her mouth hung open in helpless terror.

"Dinah! Is this your welcome to a returned sailor? Where are your mistresses? Did they hear my knock?"

Dinah cowered against the wall, subsiding gradually into a heap upon the ground, powerless to cry out, too dazed even to pray. Her scattered faculties seemed fumbling for a word of power wherewith to reinstate themselves, and avert some peril. "Jerusalem!" was the first which came to hand. Its utterance brought strength and some return of thought. It was followed by "Bress de Lord!" and then with speech restored, she clasped her hands above her head, and with all her strength cried out. "O Lordie! Take de drown man's spook away!"

The visitor turned on his heel and walked round to the front of the house, where doors and shutters stood wide open. Entering by a window open to the ground, he stood in the reception-room: it was empty, and its recesses were concealed in gloom. Nothing was clearly seen but the great white magnolia blossoms in the dim garden without, which burdened the air with their almost too luscious sweetness.

A door opened behind him and the mistress entered, followed by her daughter carrying a lamp. The young man turned eagerly, and the light falling on his features betrayed a shade of disappointment passing across them as he recognised the ladies.

"Is Lina from home?" he asked. "But, mother, at least you can welcome me home in the meantime. What! Not a word! No kiss even for your long-lost son-in-law! Surely that is carrying your New England reserve too far."

"Welcome if you will, then, lad! I wish you nought but good. I always liked you well; and you have done nothing to make me change. But oh! if it had been His will, I would fain you had never returned, seeing you have stayed so long."

She laid her hand upon his open palm. It was cold and nerveless, and her eyes were full of tears.

The young man would have clasped the fingers, but their dullness stole into his heart, and the tremor of her voice filled him with sickening forebodings.

"Lina! Where is Lina? Tell me quick! Has anything come to her?"

"She is gone."

"Dead, do you mean to say?"

"The same to you, lad, as if she were. She is gone from you for ever."

"Hush, mother!" said the daughter. "Remember we agreed to tell him nothing."

"Millicent! Is it you who say such things? What do you mean? Would you keep me from my wife?"

"She is gone; and you must never see her more," said Millicent.

"I must! and will! and shall!"

"You are not the man, then," cried the elder woman, "that I take you for. I tell you, lad, the sight of you would kill her!"

"Why so? What have you told her about me? What has she done? Or what do you say that *I* have done?"

"Neither of you has done aught amiss, lad--of that I am right sure."

"What then? What is the matter?"

"Let it rest, lad. It is God's will. Be brave. Be a man, and bear it."

"Bear what? What is it I must bear? You have no right to doubt my courage. Why will you not speak? I demand to be told all."

"Oh lad!--my poor, poor lad!" sobbed the old woman. "Why will you be so set? It is to save your own poor heart that we would keep you in the dark; for what we should have to tell can bring you nought but sorrow--a sorrow without a remedy."

"Have no fear for me. Speak! I can carry my load, whatever it may be. What is your mystery? Where is Lina?"

"Gone, lad! Have done with her."

"Gone?--dead? No! You do not mean that she is dead. You would have told me that at once. What is it that you mean? Say! Is my Lina not alive? Answer me."

"She lives," the mother answered, with a groan. "There! Nay, it is useless to press me. I tell you she is gone."

"Gone! Would you insinuate shame against my wedded wife? Unnatural!--against your own sweet daughter? Where has she gone?--and when?--and how?--I am after her. Tell me quick!"

"You cannot go to her, Joseph. She is far away. And"--laying her hand on his arm--"at least I can tell you this, and assure you with all my heart; there is nought to blush for. She was your faithful wife. No shame can light on her, or upon you."

"*Was*, you say?"

"Yes, lad; all's over now."

"What do you mean?"

"She is married--married again."

"Another man's wife? I do not believe you. What man would dare----? I'll have his life! But it is not true. Lina never would desert me."

"Word came that you were lost. Remember that. Pieces of the wreck were picked up at sea. And Lina--she nearly lost her reason. We thought that she would die."

"But I wrote--wrote several times. Do you mean that she did not get my letters?" and the young man paced the room in vehement disorder. "You knew I was alive! I can see that you did. You were expecting me! I can guess it from your delay in letting me in. You would have kept me out altogether if you had dared! I am sure of it by your behaviour. Only you were afraid of a public scandal."

"I did, and I was, lad; and it is yourself would grieve the most, if a word were to light on the good name of the woman you vowed to love and honour."

"The woman who deserts me for another man! But still she is mine! She cannot be another's. Give her back! Give up the name of her betrayer. Who is he? Where are they? Speak!"

The mother had sunk into a chair, her arms propped upon her knees, covering her face and sobbing wildly, while Millicent bent down and strove to soothe her.

"Speak, woman! speak!" he shouted.

"Have you no pity?" It was Millicent who spoke.

"What pity are you showing now to me? Give back my wife! Where have you hidden her? And this man----? She has left me, has she? But *he* shall not have her! If I had him by the throat----!" and he clenched his teeth in fury.

"Lina never left you. You might know it. You should blush to have thought it. If ever woman was devoted to a man, it was our Lina. When word came that you were lost, she fell senseless on the floor. It was weeks before she recovered her reason; and even then it seemed doubtful if she would survive. We took her North as soon as we dared move her, and in the bracing air and change of scene it seemed as if the vehemence of her grief had spent itself; but the old self seemed to have gone from her as well. She moved about a listless white-faced shadow, indifferent to life and everything. It was heartbreaking to see her--and she not yet eighteen! And mother and I, we were beside ourselves with anxiety. She appeared too feeble to bring back here, and we feared the sight of the familiar scenes would revive her grief, and drive her mad, or kill her. And so, when a gentleman grew interested in her, and slid into a kind of pitiful intimacy that seemed to soothe her, we thanked God for raising us up a consoler. And when, by-and-by, he asked her to marry him, mother and I persuaded her to listen, for we thought that new duties and a new life would draw her thoughts away from her great sorrow, and bring her peace. It was fifteen months, or more, from the time the news reached us of your loss, when she was married; so you have no call to say that her memory was short, or that her love was light to come and light to go. She loved you very truly, and she cherishes your memory yet."

"What did she say when she received my letters?"

"She has received none of them. When mother and I got home after her marriage, we found one awaiting us here. We opened it and we read it, and we burned it--though it went to our hearts to do so."

"What right had you to open a letter to my wife? what right to intercept it?"

"The right of her nearest to guard poor Lina's peace. What good would it have done you if we had given it to her? No doubt she would have left her husband; but that would not have given her back to *you*. You know her as well as I do. You know that she would not have looked you in the face after having given herself to another. She would have pined away for shame; or, more likely, she would have gone mad."

"Yes, lad," put in the mother, "you must take your trouble on your own back, unless you would destroy the woman you bound yourself to defend. You must go away and never let her know you are alive. I make no question but she would leave her present husband without a word; but think of yourself!

Could *you* take her to your bosom out of another man's arms? Could she ever be the same to you as she was before?"

"Perhaps--perhaps--I do not know."

"And think of her! How could she live beneath your looks of always remembering reproach?"

"At least I can promise never to say a word. I would not reproach her."

"Not in words, I well believe, lad. But the reproach unspoken of a wounded love will out in many a tone and look, without our knowing. And then, there is the world. How could my girl hold up her head among honest women? Their pity would be harder even than their scorn to bear. Lina would die of shame. Oh, lad! be generous, as I know you are able to be. I know you for a brave true man; and when the first smart is past, you will have pity for the girl you loved, and who loved you well. You will spare her weakness, and let your own brave strong heart contain its grief in silence. You do not know her name or where she dwells, and you will not attempt to seek her."

The young man smothered a mighty sob, which nearly rent his breast asunder, and drew his hand roughly across his eyes to clear their gathering dimness. He turned and went, without a word of leave-taking. The elasticity was gone out of his step. His shoulders were bowed as though they bore a burden. His face was drawn, and aged, and faded. His very soul seemed crushed. Without another word he stole away out into the night, where no eye could pry into his sorrow.

Next day he left New Orleans, and forsook the sea. He returned to his native province, and, entering on a new career, strove to absorb himself in its new interests, and forget the past. He prospered, but he never forgot; or, if he did, the faculty of loving seemed to have died out of him in the meanwhile. In five-and-twenty years from the day he lost his wife, no other woman had been able to awaken even a passing interest in his mind.

CHAPTER II.

CLAM BEACH.

The Chowder House at Clam Beach is not a giant among the hotels which line the Atlantic coast. It is designed to accommodate only a hundred guests, and even at the height of the season it refuses to stretch its capacity beyond a hundred and fifty. It stands upon a solitary shore, is some miles from the nearest railway, and shows nothing from its windows but the tumbling line of surf and the daily procession of cloud and sunshine across a boundless stretch of sea and sand.

It is a three-storeyed building encased in wooden galleries, which form outside corridors on the different floors; and it forms three sides of a square, enclosing to the back a sheltered tennis-lawn for those who would avoid the bluster of the keen sea-breeze.

The place is resorted to by families with a juvenile division, whose nurses and small fry burrow in the sand which comes up to the very doorsteps. It makes no pretence to fashion. The guests feel at liberty to be happy, each in his own favourite dress and manner, without fear of being compromised. The young bathe in the surf and walk or ride on the sands all day; and after the Yankee supper of meats, fruit, and tea, which takes place at seven, make themselves gay with dances and singing: while the seniors stroll together in groups, or sit apart, acquiescing in the American law of life, which gives the world to the young, and places the middle-aged with the elders on the shelf. The old may work, if so is their good pleasure, but it is only the lads and lasses who are to play.

It was early afternoon, in the very hottest of the day. The first bell for dinner had rung, and the guests were streaming towards the house from every point along the shore; while the most hungry, already arrived, loitered on the galleries, and counted the minutes till the dining-room should be thrown open.

The omnibus from the station, jolting round the corner, and drawing up before the door, afforded a pleasing diversion from the yearnings of appetite. It brought the newspapers of the day; and more, it brought new guests, who, busied in alighting and claiming their luggage, formed a subject for observation to the idle eyes above, unintroduced as yet, and therefore at liberty to stare their fill with all the impertinent curiosity at their disposal.

The ladies counted the boxes on the roof, and turned away with a sniff. Even at Clam Beach, with its freedom from dress parade, the number of trunks is taken as a criterion of "standing," and certain ladies of grand manner from Boston are even suspected of bringing empty ones to support their position.

The men, toothpick in mouth, continued to stare. There were two pretty faces visible beneath the flapping brims of broad seaside hats,--one violet-eyed, with masses of sunny brown hair; the other blond, with eyes like the forget-me-not,--and they could study them without prejudice or offence just then. Later, when they met in the parlours above, it would be different.

Presently the hotel cart trotted up with a number of trunks. A slight "Ah!" of satisfaction spread itself on the air, and the ladies resumed their attitude of observation. They were not going to be compromised after all, it seemed, by the presence of fellow-guests without ostensible movable property, and forthwith they began to note the value and fashion of each article of the feminine newcomers' wardrobe, and the general look of the men. One of these appeared about thirty, available for flirtation and social uses; while the other was older, with a suspicion of grey in the short close-cut whisker--a florid and well-fed man, and seemingly well to do, which was a point in favour of his female following: and a point of some sort is needed where available men to marriageable girls stand in the proportion of only two to five.

Two oldish ladies brought up the number of the arrivals to six; but as they were dressed in the ordinary manner of the period, nobody noticed them much. They were mere furniture, intended to remain in corners, and be sat beside when younger women, finding themselves neglected, chose to assume demureness under the wing of a chaperon.

"Two trunks. Those! Valise, handbag, rugs, and umbrellas." It was the younger man who was addressing the porter.

"Oh, Peter!" cried the oldest lady, "have you my parrysol?--and my book?--and my scent-bottle?--and my spectacle-case? Where can they all be?"

"You've just left them behind you, mother, as usual. You would have left yourself, I do believe, if I had not been at your elbow."

"What am I to do for want of my parrysol? Between the hot sun and the sea air, every bit of colour will be eaten out of my blue ribbons, and my face just brandered like a raw beef-steak. I wonder if the little things can have gotten into my pockets!" And so saying, she stepped forth upon the gravel, where elbow-room was free, shook out her skirts, and proceeded to dive down deep into apertures she wot of in all parts of her circumference.

"What's this?" she cried, sinking over the elbow into a pocket on the far-off side. "What can it be?" And the eyes and eyeglasses in the galleries were turned in her direction; while Peter, half wroth and half amused, stood waiting the end of her search.

"It's terrible hard to grip. But there! Now! I've cornered it at last. Can it be livin', I wonder? The way it runs about! And I canna just lay finger on it."

"A mouse, mother, is it?" He was growing cross and sarcastic under the observation of the loungers. "Out with it! Here's a terrier ready to snap it up."

"Peter Wilkie, hold your peace! Would ye make fun of your own mother, and all thae impident Yankees looking on? Think shame! Hey! here it is at last, the bothersome thing!" And out it came, proving to be only a large-sized peppermint-drop.

"Toot! that's not what I was looking for. Here, my dear!" and without more ado she popped it into the open mouth of a small boy who stood by gaping at her in her search, to his complete confusion and the increased diversion of the gallery.

"See there, Peter! If that's no' the parrysol after all, tied up with the umbrellies! Just where it should be! And me hunting for it everywhere! I wonder you didn't see it! And here's the specs and the scent-bottle all the time in the ridicule at my side! Wonders will never cease. As for the book, it'll turn up ere I want it; and if anybody took it, they'll be little made up, for it's just Beattie's Lectures on the Ten Commandments, and very hard upon the sin of stealing. And, Peter, be sure and make the landlord give us rooms upon the first floor. I *can-not* be climbing stairs--it brings on the palpitations."

Meanwhile the other tenants of the omnibus had alighted and entered the house. "A man with a sickly wife and a couple of daughters," was the verdict upon the party, which was only rectified by reference to the house-register after they had catalogued themselves--"Joseph Naylor, Mrs Caleb Naylor, and the Misses Naylor, all of Jones's Landing, Upper Canada."

"Oh, girls, I am exhausted! Open the windows and the trunks. Hartshorn and sal-volatile! I shall faint--I am sure I shall faint. Margaret, get ready to go down with your uncle. Lucy, my child, you must remain with me."

"Stuff and nonsense, Maria!" said the uncle. They were being shown their rooms up-stairs. "You have only to exert yourself. That's all you require to set you up. And of course you must come down to dinner. The sight of so many strangers will do you good, and we shall want your help to make up our minds about the company."

Mrs Naylor shook her head in plaintive toleration. It was not to be expected that coarse-fibred masculinity should comprehend the susceptibility of her delicate nerves. She half-closed her eyes and sank into a chair, with every appearance of taking up her quarters for good--unless, indeed, she should have to be laid upon the adjoining bed.

Joseph, standing impatiently without, grew uneasy, as perhaps was intended. He was of an anxious temper, fussy as well as kind. The responsibility of having a delicate lady on his hands oppressed him. He had groaned under the load for years, but he had not got used to it. It oppressed him ever the more, the longer he endured it, and he was overridden by the whims and complaints of this relict of his deceased brother, even more than if she had been wife of his own.

"Pray try, sister--try. It is for your health we are here, you know. It will be distressing if you begin by taking to your bed. I feel confident that a morsel of dinner and a glass of sparkling wine will do you good."

I will not say that it was the suggestion of the wine which induced Mrs Naylor to change her purpose; it may only have been willingness to yield to entreaty. At any rate, she let herself be persuaded, though not too easily, and eventually went downstairs with the rest.

At dinner they shared a table with their fellow-travellers of the omnibus, and found Mr Wilkie and his mother already placed when they entered.

"Mother," Peter had been saying, "you will have to behave here, or you will compromise me before all those Toronto people. If they carry back a tale of queer doings on our part, you will find it harder than ever to get into society when we go home. There is Mrs Judge Petty with her son and daughter, and there Colonel and Mrs Carraway, and the Vice-Chancellor Chickenpips! Mind what you are about. This is not the Gallowgate of Glasgow--remember that! If they see you biting your bread or eating with your knife, you're done for; and so am I."

"Peter Wilkie, I wonder ye can have the heart to be speaking like that to your dying mother!--bringing on the palpitations worse than ever. Oh, my heart! it's just thumping. If I did take lodgers at one time--ay, and turn the mangle with my own hands--whose sake was it done for? Tell me that. I wonder where the money would have come from to pay for your fine edication if I had chosen to sit and drink my tea in the afternoons like a feckless leddy, as I might have done! It wasn't your bankrupt father, danderin' about the doors hand-idle, that could have helped you. I just slaved with that mangle and the lodgers to bring up my boay; and now, when he is in a splendid way of doing, this is the thanks he gives me--to cast the Gallowgate up to me! As if it wasna you, and your father before you, that brought me down to that! Think shame of yourself, Peter Wilkie!" And the big round tears came rattling in a very hailstorm out of the old blue eyes, leaving watercourses among her ribbons, and mingling with the gravy in her plate, till the son felt like a brute--or at least he should have felt so; and he certainly feared that he must appear like one in the eyes of any fellow-guest who might observe him.

The entrance of the Naylors made a welcome diversion. As they took their places the old woman's tears dried up of themselves, her eyes being withdrawn from the inward contemplation of her own distresses to the lace cap of Mrs Naylor and the gowns of her daughters. Unconsciously she sat up more squarely in her chair, prinked out her cap-strings, and wondered if Mrs Naylor's hair could be all her own; while her son and the gentleman exchanged an observation on the journey they had made together.

Mrs Naylor was not only of the Provinces, but provincial at that. Like other "leading ladies" of Jones's Landing, she was wont to inform strangers that she was "very exclusive," with the gratifying result of taking away their breath; though perhaps, if she had but known, it was the stupendous conceit which could imagine herself or her circle in the smallest degree desirable, rather than the splendour of her position which astonished them. She had no small opinion of her "position," but, like other rural great ones, she bowed in her heart before the superiority of dwellers in the capital. There was a grandeur in their way of accepting her pretensions, while setting them calmly aside, which filled her with admiring awe on her rare visits to Toronto--made her rave about its elegance, and try to play off in Jones's Landing some of the mannerisms she had found so impressive. And here it may be observed that, in its way, Toronto is a capital, even as New York is, or London, and quite as accustomed as either to put on metropolitan airs, so far as circumstances permit; and seeing that all mankind are made of one kind of clay, there may be less difference in the spirit which animates the small community and the great one than would appear. A cock-boat is built of the same materials as a man-of-war, and it is floated and steered in accordance with the same laws of nature.

At a distant table Mrs Naylor descried Mrs Justice Petty, Mrs Vice-Chancellor Chickenpip, and Mrs Carraway--the very cream of Toronto society. Ice-cream, alas! they were likely to prove to Mrs Naylor, as she did not know them, and they made a point of not thawing to unknown fellow-country-women whom they met in American hotels--it being difficult to shake them off afterwards, especially the undesirable ones. So far, indeed, did those ladies' prudence carry them, that they would only bathe at eccentric hours and in secretly arranged parties. The very sea should not receive them in the same embrace with persons from Canada who were not in Society. As for Americans, it did not matter: they might never meet them again, and Americans are held to be a peculiar people, without social degrees or defined lines of demarcation. Everybody among them may be anybody, and each is expected to have a spice of everything. Among them, vulgarity, if they have any, is overlooked. They are generally amusing, often rich, and cannot compromise a Canadian.

Mrs Naylor's eye, surveying the company, lighted on her distinguished compatriots. She knew them, although she had not the happiness of being acquainted with them--a humbling thought, which made her approach with more meekness than otherwise she might have felt, the two people from Toronto who shared her table. If not the rose, they at least grew near it, and might--who knew?--be woven into a link of connection with the queen of flowers. She addressed a polite observation to the old lady, who, accepting it as a tribute to her clever son and her own good looks, responded affably, as not unwilling to confer the favour of her notice, though aware that it was a thing of value.

And so it came about that, when dinner was over, the Naylor party and the Wilkies had coalesced, and strolled together to a shady corner of the galleries, where broad awnings, flapping in fitful air-currents, lent a little freshness to the languor of the hot and drowsy afternoon.

CHAPTER III.

THE FIRST EVENING.

When the sweltering hours of afternoon have passed on westward, and the shadows creep out to meet the coming twilight in the east, there is an arousing in the world comparable to the quickening which passes across it at the opening of each new day. The air, too languid, an hour since, to lift the drooping streamer on the flag-staff, awakens into flutterings which set the aspen-leaves in the shrubbery spinning gleefully upon their slender stalks. The watch-dog rattling his chain emerges from his kennel, stretching and blinking, and yawning his formidable jaws. The interest of living steals slowly back on him, and ere long he is amusing himself with a half-gnawed bone, his eyes fixed upon the kitchen-door, whence supper and the cook are wont to visit him.

There are stirrings and rustlings in the long silent passages and chambers of the hotel. The life of the inmates, which had burned low, like charcoal-embers in the thick hot stillness, lights up in the eddies of cooler air which flutter in, and brightens into flame. The sleepers draw themselves together where they lie on swing, in hammock, on couch, or deeply cushioned chair, and open their eyes and start and are awake, inhale the freshness of the sea-salt air, and the house is alive once more with the stirring of its inmates, like a clock which had run down, but is now wound up and set agoing.

Old Mrs Wilkie had been surprised by sleep as she lay back in a long cane chair, preliminary to getting up and seeking the privacy of her chamber. Her feet had been raised on the further end of the seductive invention for barely a second, when, with a sigh, her head fell backward, leaving the lips apart, and plunging her in deep sweet gurgling slumber, which echoed purlingly along the silent gallery, like sounds of hidden brooks in shady dells.

She started now, and, wheeling round, sat bolt-upright, in haste to hide among her skirts the broad prunella shoes which had stood up before her like a massive screen, concealing her foreshortened figure from intrusive eyes.

"Peter Wilkie! are you sleeping? Come here," were the first words she spoke on opening her eyes. There was crossness in her voice, and her face was aflush with anger, or perhaps with lingering sleep. "I wish you would speak to that impertinent Yankee woman over there. What business has she looking at me like that? It's my feet she's trying to see, I do believe."

"They're big enough to be plainly seen without much trying, mother. But never mind, I'll back them to gang their ain gate against hers or anybody's.

Why did you not go to your room, as I advised you, instead of exhibiting yourself like a sleeping beauty before the whole house?"

"I just fell asleep before I knew; and it's like your father's son to be jawing and jeering when I'm too poorly to take my own part," and she pressed her side. "Sleeping beauty, quothy! It'll be telling ye, my man, if any scart of a wife ye may pick up in this unwholesome country keeps her looks half as well when she comes to my time of life;" and having secured the last word, she withdrew to smooth her tumbled hair and prepare for the next meal.

There was a general rolling up of awnings and opening of shutters all over the house. Doors and windows were thrown open, and whisperings from the sea stole in everywhere, bringing freshness and gaiety where sloth and prostration had brooded all the afternoon. The sounds of laughter and tripping feet echoed on the stairs, and presently the whole body of guests come out from supper were assembled in the parlours. There were three parlours, connected with each other by folding-doors. Only one was carpeted, to be ready for rainy days at the end of the season. The boards of the other two were bare, like the holystoned deck of a steamer; and, with their open windows descending to the floor, they had the appearance of sheltered continuations of the gallery without, rather than of rooms, they were so sweet and fresh and spacious.

Round the pianos, or rather one of them, the crowd gathered. A Bostonian, the pet of the ladies and the aversion of the other young men, seated himself before it and began to play. He played, as the male amateur is wont to play, with abundant sound--eliciting admiring whispers as to the energy of his touch, and acquitting himself successfully, though by no means with the brilliancy he himself supposed. Ere long he slid into a waltz, and then the crowd broke up into its component parts. Those who could find a partner began to dance, those who desired one looked about or waited to be asked, while the elders withdrew to the carpeted drawing-room.

Those first to reach it having secured the rocking-chairs, the remainder had to sit still,--all, that is, but Miss Maida Springer, a school-ma'am, the gossips said, from Vermont--a lady of questionable youth but indubitable independence of character, who tilted her chair till its back touched the wall, and swung her feet in a plenitude of sedentary exercise such as no rocker could afford.

Mrs Judge Petty was one of the first to reach the drawing-room and install herself in a comfortable place. Having done so, she had leisure to look round and consider how the places near her should be filled. Her eye lighted on Mrs Wilkie drifting doubtfully on the stream, and, fixing her with an encouraging smile, drew her forward, and landed her with a turn of the eyelid on a sofa at her elbow.

Mrs Naylor followed close upon her new acquaintance, and Mrs Petty, feeling no desire to know *her*, would fain have staved her off with a chilling stare; but Mrs Naylor could play burr on occasion, and knew how to disregard what it would be inconvenient to see. She stuck to her friend, and made small-talk whilst settling herself by her side; and Mrs Wilkie, though eager to meet the advances of the more worshipful lady, was too unskilful to refrain from answering her assiduous companion. It was tantalising. Circumstances through life had kept her far off from the judges and magnates of her native land; and now, when she was abroad, and at last in clover--when great ones were actually seeking her acquaintance--to think that a quite ordinary person should intrusively interfere! It made her cross, and her replies grew short and dry; but, alas! to no good purpose--for though Mrs Naylor could be silenced by taciturnity, Mrs Petty had turned away her head in the meantime, and was interesting herself in other things.

Mrs Wilkie flushed and fretted; Mrs Naylor sat and bided her time. She had two girls to bring out and marry well--enterprises in which patience and ability to eat humble-pie speed better than more brilliant qualities. She sat by Mrs Wilkie, keeping her company, though neither spoke. Their eyes were occupied with the moving crowd of dancers in the distance, as they whirled and floated on the tide of sound.

After a while Mrs Petty turned round to her neighbour and observed, "I think I see Mr Wilkie--your son, is he not?--dancing with my daughter Ann. A good height, are they not, for each other? They really look very well."

"Most girls look well dancing with my Peter--Mr Wilkie, I ought to say, for we can't look on a young man in his fine position as just a boy; though, to be sure, he will always be a boy to me. Eh!--the trouble I had with him in his teething! I can never forget that, and the day we put on his first pair of little trousers. I made them myself out of a bit of black-and-red tartan. And now, to see him 'dancing in the hall,' as the song says, with all the finest girls in the room just scuffling to get a catch of him."

Mrs Petty was scarcely gratified at the remark, but she was amused; and as we grow older on this humdrum planet, to be amused befalls one so seldom that it compensates for much, even for a lack of proper respect--so she acquiesced.

"Yes," she said, "Mr Petty--Judge Petty, you know, my husband--says he thinks highly of your son, and expects him to do very well. I too have met him, and like the little I have seen; and now apparently he has made the acquaintance of Ann, and they seem to get on together very nicely."

"Oh yes," chuckled the mother, "he's a great boy with the girls, our Peter. They're all pulling caps to see who's going to get him. I just----"

"Hm!" coughed Mrs Petty, in haste to interrupt before anything worse had been said of the girls, among whom her own daughter seemed audaciously to be included. "Oh yes, an excellent young man. I have scarcely met him, but I hope to see more of him next winter, and I am very pleased to meet his mother."

Whereat the other bridled and was happy. How well it would read in her next letter to her husband--hid away somewhere in Scotland, and never alluded to--to mention Mr Justice Petty and his family among her intimate friends!

"Don't you think my daughter Ann is looking her best this evening?" the younger mother went on. "So animated. She is perhaps too tranquil in general. 'Statuesque' was how young Lord Norman described her, when he passed through Toronto last spring. And really she is clever, though ill-natured people say she has no conversation. When she gets hold of a clever man who can understand, see! she positively rattles."

"Oh yes, Peter generally makes the girls rattle. He's very quick about sounding them. Terrible empty, though, he says he generally finds them;" which was a remark she should have spared her new friend, in view of the elation she felt in making the acquaintance; but Peter was her monomania. With his name on her lips, the words would come of themselves, without judgment or consideration.

"There is my son Walter, too," Mrs Petty continued, taking no notice. "Dancing, I declare, instead of smoking out of doors. A positive achievement on the part of that young lady, if she only knew. A very handsome girl, and nicely dressed; but I do not seem to have observed her before--must have arrived to-day."

"So she did," answered Mrs Wilkie. "That's--dear me! how bad my memory is growing!"

"Miss Naylor," volunteered her mother. "Niece of Joseph Naylor of Jones's Landing."

"The great lumberman? In--deed!" said Mrs Petty, interested and impressed. "I did not hear of her arrival. I wonder if *he* is coming! The richest bachelor in Upper Canada, I understand. It is a risky business, but still----. One likes to see a celebrity."

"He is here," his sister-in-law observed. "We arrived this afternoon."

Mrs Petty turned her eyes, and for the first time permitted them to be seen resting on the stranger, addressing her with much politeness at the same time. "Then perhaps you are related to the beautiful girl who is dancing with my son?"

"She is my daughter Margaret. I am Mrs Caleb Naylor."

"So happy to know you, Mrs Naylor," and forthwith the mothers conversed freely across Mrs Wilkie and over her head, on subjects in which it was impossible for her to join, though many were her abortive attempts to put in an oar. Even Mrs Naylor, whose chit-chat she had stifled with her taciturnity half an hour before, was now grown deaf and unresponsive to anything she could say.

CHAPTER IV.

THE PERILS OF SURF-BATHING.

When the day is young and the sky is blue, with just a flake or two of cloud low down on the horizon; when the sea, in purple slumber like a dreaming child, is brightened by the flickering glance and shadow on its rippling swell--and the surf, cresting itself in a wall of translucent green, leaps up and curls and topples over, crumbling in snow-white foam upon the sand; when the breeze, still gleeful with the memory of dew and starlit revels overnight, flits fresh and crisp beneath the early sunshine,--it is then that it is good to be a dweller by the shore: to spring from the unconsciousness of sleep into the luxury of sentient being, with softly fanning airs curling about the limbs, and wakening in them all their suppleness and strength.

Obeying the summons of the early gong, the young and vigorous of the guests of the hotel had hastened to the bathing-houses on the beach, and now came forth a gay and motley company. They were dressed in suits of red, blue, orange, green, and grey, with hats of straw or caps of oilskin, or only falling hair by way of head-dress. White ankles twinkled all along the sand, and the air was musical with laughter, as they scampered down and halted by the margin of the white sea-foam,--ladies and men distinguishable only by their hair or beard, or by less or greater bulk. They arranged themselves like a necklace of brightly coloured beads, where great and small alternated with each other. Each smaller figure was attended by one of the sturdy kind, as though they were about to dance. The surf along that coast breaks in such massive billows, that the little and the weak can scarce bear up alone against the whelming rush, or keep their footing. They are liable to be thrown down by an advancing roller, turned over when it breaks, sucked outward in the reflux, and carried beyond their depth.

The party joined hands, and then stepped out into the foam, a string of forty beads, to bind the bosom of the next big wave, so green and smooth and glassy; but as it yet came on, so huge and impressive with its crest of foam, like the tossing manes of Pharaoh's chariot-horses, the line outstepping stopped and wavered and bent, as one panic-stricken near the centre suddenly bounded back, and left the wings of the line turned sidewise and irresolute, while the wave was sweeping up indifferent to the doubts and fears of mortals. It swept upon the wings all unprepared to meet it, lifting them from their feet and throwing them down, and dabbling them in the wreck of foam and sand.

"Oh, Lucy Naylor! that was not fair!--to spring back suddenly and leave us in the lurch!" rang out from several pairs of feminine lips. "I will not bathe with you again, if you go on so." But the laughter of those who were amused at the disaster overbore the displeasure of the remonstrants; and it being Lucy's first morning, she was forgiven on promising to be more courageous.

The line formed up once more, and stepped out steadily to meet the next invader; and on he came, a smooth green hill, with the frothing and hissing water gathering on the summit like the gnashing teeth of an advancing monster. The line stood still, with spreading feet, bent knee, and breath held in. The monster was upon them, and with a little cry from here and there along the line, smothered and drowned and overwhelmed in the hissing deluge as it heaved above them, and with a thunderous roar, it broke up upon the shore behind them, and then drew back again in hurrying, seething foam, and left the line still standing. And then there was a sob or two, and a cry, followed by laughter and little screams of delight The cool sea water had drenched their shrinking frames, the saltness prickled exhilaratingly on the skin, and it was, as some one said, "just altogether too delightful."

Again the line was formed, and again. Even the timid ones had grown courageous. The least expert had learned to shoulder and resist the coming waves. The world was all coolness and freshness and sparkle, and each new wave was plunged into with a relish keener than the last, when came a new disturbance or alarm, more pressing and more vehement than even the onslaught of the billows upon the inexperienced. It sounded from the shore, a voice addressing them in accents shrill and clamorous. They ceased their sport and turned, and beheld a figure with flushed cheeks, no bonnet, her hair disordered, and her cap askew, with ribbons fluttering wildly in the breeze.

"Peter Wilkie!" it cried--"Peter Wilkie! Do ye not hear your mother crying to ye, fit to crack her voice? Let go that woman's hand, and come out ower this moment!--Peter! Do you hear me? Leave go, and come out ower. To think that I should live to see the proper up-bringing I have spared no pains to give ye, circumvented and brought to nothing by a set of shameless hempies like this!--and you just danderin' in the middle of them, like a fool goin' to the correction of the stocks!"

Mr Peter passed through many phases of feeling while he was being addressed. First, he was ashamed for his mother's sake. He would fain have taken no notice, and plunged with his companions into the coming wave, in hopes that others would do the same, and every one's attention be withdrawn. Then he grew angry, and endeavoured to laugh off the intrusion as a quaint absurdity; but as the old lady's voice rose higher, and an audible titter ran along the line on either side of him, he realised that he must close the scene at once, on any terms. To outface the clamour was manifestly impossible, while to yield would at least bring the scolding to an end. With a shrug and a scowl, which he strove to hide behind a cough, and an acid smile, he stepped ashore, took his mother's hand, all dripping as he was, and led her away behind the bathing-houses, where, let us hope, an understanding and a reconciliation were effected.

The interest of the bathers being thus disturbed, many began to feel chilly and to think they had had enough. Only the few who were good swimmers cared to remain, and these struck out beyond the ruin of breakers, to disport themselves above the placid depths beyond.

In the unbroken water outside, they could frolic at will, diving, floating, treading water, or swimming further seaward. Naylor, the uncle of his nieces, who have been mentioned, was one of the eagerest of all. A man no longer young, but with no sign of coming age save a thinning of the hair above his temples. Well nourished and prosperous of aspect, and five feet nine or so in height; broad-shouldered, muscular, and active, with cheery grey eyes, and a face burnt red by the sun. His spirits rose with the increasing coolness of the water, as he swam out and out; and from the sedate middle-aged person he had been on shore, he seemed changed into a hilarious youth among his new associates, challenging those near him to strange feats and gambols, laughing and shouting like a schoolboy.

Suddenly, with a cry, he threw up his hands, and sank beneath the surface.

"Not a bad imitation of a drowning man; but I wish he would not do it out here, where the water is deep. It isn't half funny. It spoils one's stroke, and makes me feel heavy and weak," some one said.

"I am not sure that it was imitation," answered another--a lady this one. "He may have a cramp. Watch when he rises."

Presently his head emerged gasping from the depths, and Miss Hillyard, the lady who had spoken, swam to him, and was able to get her fingers into his hair, just as he was beginning to sink again, and lifted his head an inch or two for a moment, calling wildly on the others at the same time to come to her assistance.

"Strike out!" she cried to the drowning man, tugging his hair again, and feeling her own poise seriously endangered by the effort. "What is the matter with you?"

"Cramp," he gasped. "Help me on my back. Perhaps I may manage to float."

"Help! Mr Sefton, help!" screamed the lady; and Mr Sefton, who was hurrying forward, was able to get a hand under the sinking man's chin on the other side, before he had drawn his other would-be rescuer under.

"Hold on now, Miss Hillyard! Don't hurry. Be calm. Steady yourself. Keep cool. We'll manage it. Trust to the water.... Good! He is up. Have a care, now. He may clutch without meaning it. Keep clear of his arms.... Steady, friend. Can't you do something for yourself?"

"I can't. Help me on my back. I cannot strike out one bit. I can hardly straighten my leg. Ugh!... Never fear, madam, I won't lay hold on you. Can you help me on my back, do you think? Never mind if you can't do it. Let go if you feel yourself sinking. One is enough to go to the bottom."

With teeth tight set, he straightened out his limbs, and held them motionless; and by-and-by they succeeded in getting him on his back, and began to tow and steer him to the shore.

Fortunately the tide had not yet turned. It was rising still; so the water helped them on their long and tardy voyage.

It was an arduous and a tedious task, and but for the tranquil coolness of the man they were trying to save, it would have been beyond their power, as they had been a long way out when the accident occurred. As they approached the surf-line, however, their labour grew lighter, and presently the heaving swell caught hold of them and swung them forward with accelerating speed, as though the hungry ocean, balked of his intended prey, had grown eager to reject the victim he had failed to drown. Surging and swinging on the translucent tide, they were borne forward more and more swiftly, and were shot at last through the curling and overarching bank of surf into shallow water, where the crowd, which had been watching on the beach, ran in and dragged the exhausted trio ashore.

"Uncle!" cried his nieces, laying hold on him, all dripping as he was, and bestowing hugs of congratulation. "You venturesome old man! How rash to go swimming out so far, this very first morning!"

"I should have been done for, if it had not been for this young lady. I would wish to thank you, madam, if I could find words; but when it is one's life that has been saved, one does not know how properly to express it."

"Pray say nothing," said Miss Hillyard, looking calm and handsome even in her dripping bathing-dress, her arms so white and strong and shapely folded on her breast, and the long dark hair hanging like a mantle down her back. "Do not say a word. Any one who was able to swim must have done the same. I am glad that I was near at the moment, and able to be of use."

And then the bathers dispersed to get dried and dressed, leaving the beach to the waves and the sea-birds undisturbed.

Joseph Naylor was an object of interest for the remainder of that day to all Clam Beach, as the man who had been all but drowned; but Miss Hillyard was the heroine for the rest of the season. She had saved a life, and the circumstances grew more marvellous from day to day, as each narrator in turn strove to give thrill to the only tale of peril he had ever assisted at; till at length the young lady, growing bored with the wondering respect it brought her, and which was far from being the form of admiration in which she took pleasure, began to deny the incident altogether, and assure people that it had never taken place.

CHAPTER V.

ROSE AND LETTICE.

However indifferent or even nauseous applause become familiar may ultimately grow, it is intensely agreeable while it is yet new. Only with time and habitude does it begin, like other sweets, to pall upon the healthy appetite. Miss Hillyard, on the day of her exploit, distinctly enjoyed the feeling that all eyes followed her, and that other conversation was hushed whenever she chose to speak. It was an ovation with which she was favoured on coming down to breakfast. Every one who knew her was waiting with congratulations to extol her pluck, and those who did not, were striving to be introduced.

Her friends felt an accession of importance in belonging to her; and Mrs Senator Deane of Indiana, under whose wing she was travelling, secured a carriage for a drive along the shore, so soon as breakfast was over, to keep the distinction of the heroine's intimacy secure in her own party.

Notoriety in a hotel, or anywhere else, grows cheap when the noted one is to be met upon the stairs and on doorsteps all day long, and can be accosted and questioned by every comer, while a morning of privacy could not fail to increase general interest in the whole party. The exploit was sure to be talked over without reserve in their absence, and on their return each member of the community would be affected with the general enthusiasm which his own contribution had done something to augment.

"Tell us all about it now, Rose, from the very beginning," cried Lettice Deane, catching both her hands, as soon as they had driven from the door. "I am dying to hear everything, now we are out of that inquisitive crowd--Yankees with their straight out questions, and Canucks with that wooden British way of theirs, staring without a wink and saying nothing, but drinking in everything with their eyes. Give me Western folks after all, say I. One knows what they are and how to deal with them from the first. These down-Easters, with their intelligence, and their conceit, and their determination to know all about it, make me feel like a potato-bug on the end of a pin, under a microscope. I like folks that are smart, but the cultured intelligence of Boston is just something too awful."

"But decent Canadians do not ask questions."

"I wish they would. They are always looking them--with eyes made round, ears erect, and mouth ajar. I'd like to shake some of them."

"Stuff! Lettie. I am Canadian, please remember."

"You are different. You have lived in Chicago; and that cures most things. But tell us now!--all about it. How did it begin?"

"Begin? Let me see. We were all out together in the deep water, having a social swim, and showing each other what we could do. Mr Sefton had just picked up a shell from the bottom--quite a pretty one, too, it seemed--and was swimming up to give it me, when we heard a cry; and when I turned round, I was just in time to see a hand disappearing under water. You can scarcely fancy the uncomfortable thrill it gave me. At once I remembered the octopus they say was cast ashore last week at St John's, with arms a yard or two long, all covered with suckers, and I began to think of cold slimy things in the water, twisting about me and pulling me down. It took all my nerve, and the certainty that if I yielded to panic, I should sink, to compose me; when bobbing up to the surface came a head of hair, not five yards off. That calmed me. It gave me something to do."

"How brave you are, Rose! With me, now, the sight of a drowning man would have scared me out of my wits."

"You cannot swim, Lettie. That is why you think so."

"And then? What did you do next?"

"As soon as I could get near enough, I got my fingers into his hair, and pulled--just a little, then slipped my hand under his shoulder. He got his face above water then, and he began to paddle with his hands."

"And were you not afraid?"

"Well, just a little bit, perhaps, at first. I dreaded his clutching at me. That would have made a finish of us both."

"And did he not? And how could you have prevented it, if he had tried?"

"He did not once attempt to clutch--seemed most careful, indeed, to keep his hands away. Lettie! He is a perfect gentleman, that man!--and brave, I am sure, He thanked me so politely--by-and-by, when he got his face clear of the water for a bit--as politely as if we had both been on dry land--for attempting to assist him; but said he thought I had better let go, as I could not possibly swim ashore with him, and he could do nothing for himself, owing to cramp in his legs. Then Sefton joined us, and together we got him on his back. You cannot imagine how cheerful and composed he was, all through. He actually smiled when our eyes met. Not a struggle did he make, or an attempt to lay hold, which made it far more possible for us to deal with him. If he *had* struggled, you know, we should certainly have been drowned, all three."

"Don't talk of it, Rose. It is just splendid the way you managed it all, and I am glad to think the man must be a pretty good sort; for you will have to know him, I suppose, after saving his life, and you will be introducing him to mother and me and Fanny. Pity he is so old. Thirty or forty, is he not, mother?"

"More'n forty, I reckon. Rising forty-five, if he wears well. But even fifty ain't old for a marrying man--if he's well off, that is. My senator was not much younger when we made it up between us. I don't hold with very young men myself. They're real hard to break in for runnin' in double harness, and the money's still to make, ginnerally speakin'. And after the girl has slaved and pinched all through her best years, helping to make the fortune, she finds herself too old when it's made to get much good out of it. Don't you be a fool, Lettie, like my sister Barbara. She vowed she'd have a man to please her eye, even if he should vex her heart.... *And* she got him! And she never had a day's peace from the week their honeymoon ended. She died a brokenhearted woman, with nary bit of life or good looks left in five years' time."

"Pshaw, mother! If you've told that story once, you've told it fifty times. The fellow I agree to take will have to be well off, as well as young and good-looking. See if he isn't!"

"You'll have to look sharp then, Lettie. After twenty-five, a girl has to take what offers, or go without."

"You shut, Fan! School-girls are growing real forward, it seems to me."

CHAPTER VI.

WITH THE SMOKERS.

Joseph Naylor found himself a notoriety for that day, as much as the heroine who had saved his life. It was notoriety, however, with a difference, as compared with hers--less incense-like and intoxicating, though perhaps more tonic.

The Hebrew prophetess makes it the culmination of Sisera's overthrow that he, a warrior, should have been done to death by a woman; and even for the non-combatant there is something ungrateful to manly pride in owing life to a member of the weaker sex. The debt is too heavy to be repaid; and it is conventionally settled that obligation between the sexes should lie the other way. It could scarcely be agreeable to his self-love to feel himself pointed out among his fellows as the man who had gone in swimming that morning, and who would have drowned himself, if a brave young lady had not gone to his rescue and fished him out.

Mrs Carraway surveyed him through her glasses in the interval between her omelet and the robin-on-toast which constituted her breakfast. The sight of a should-have-been drowned gentleman communicated a marine flavour to the little bird, suggestive of oyster-sauce with boiled turkey,--a dish which was not on the bill of fare, and therefore the more delicious. She sent her colonel, after breakfast, to make friends with the interesting creature, and get exact particulars of how it had occurred, at first hand,--rather to the botheration of that tranquil warrior, who, since he had made his home in the Colonies, had for the most part practised an affable silence. If natives who approached him were to his liking, he accepted their advances, and graciously permitted himself to be courted; if they were not, he kept stolidly oblivious of their existence, no matter how pressing their overtures of friendship might be.

It is by no means a bad way of getting easily through life, provided you can persuade people that you are worth courting. That is the difficulty. People worth knowing can generally find better sport than cultivating your Worship; but even if they do attempt it, the game will grow monotonous ere long, on the one side as well as the other. One can fancy that Royalty itself must yawn behind a fan at times, in weariness of uninterrupted adulation.

It was a bore to so reserved a gentleman as Colonel Carraway to break through his own ice; however, he lighted a cigar and strolled away to the gallery facing the north, and always shady, where inmates addicted to tobacco were wont to smoke. Naylor had arrived there before him, and stood the centre of a group in which Judge Petty and Vice-Chancellor Chickenpip vied with each other in displaying their forensic gift of unwearied question-asking--a talent which they made it manifest had not grown rusty from disuse since their elevation to the bench.

"I never experienced the sensation of drowning," the Judge was observing. "Being unable to swim, I never was in danger of it."

"And yet," said the Vice-Chancellor, with a shrug at the little paradox, and eyeing the perpetrator with condescending superiority through his spectacles, as the self-constituted wit is apt to do when his neighbour attempts a sally, "we teach our boys to swim in order to prepare them against such dangers."

"And they rashly tempt them in consequence, and so, not unfrequently, get drowned. For myself, I have all my life had a cat's antipathy to water--always excepting, of course, my morning tub."

"So your lordship's detractors of the blue-ribbon sect have sometimes insinuated," chuckled the other, delighted to be disagreeable by way of jest, however threadbare in form the jest might be. The Vice-Chancellor owed his reputation for smartness to his talent for ill-nature. The dullest can appreciate malice, while wit which is merely sportive requires a sense of humour to understand it.

The Judge was familiar with the idiosyncrasy of his learned brother. "What need one expect from a pig but a grunt!" was his inward exclamation; but he was wise enough not to give it utterance. He merely moved nearer to Naylor, thereby half turning his back upon the other.

"I have always felt curious," he said, "to know what drowning, or, indeed, dying in any form, could be like--without personal experiment, that is. How did it feel, Mr Naylor? What were your sensations?"

"It did not get the length of drowning with me this time. I was a deal too busy struggling for my life, I can tell you, to take much heed of sensations. When at last I got my nose above water, and felt the young lady's fingers twisted in my hair, she was behaving in such splendid style that I could think of nothing but her efforts to help me. If she had not kept cool, you know, instead of drawing me up she would have been drawn down herself; and, crippled and sinking as I was, I could have done nothing to save her. My mind was completely absorbed in watching her efforts, admiring her nerve, and wondering if she would really succeed in keeping afloat. As for saving me, I did not think it possible; for, all the time, that racking cramp kept dragging my leg together, in spite of my straining efforts to stretch it, and drawing me to the bottom like tons of lead. Those cramps are hideous things; and then, after she and Mr Sefton had taken me in tow, and the anxiety for her safety grew less absorbing, the drowning man's instinct of clutching came upon me, and it was all I could do to keep still, and let myself be saved. You are perfectly right, Judge, to keep clear of the possibility of such an experience; but still, this experience was quite different from the feeling of drowning--the helpless struggling and sinking down and away, the yielding of what sustains you on every side, till the idea of up and down is lost in dizziness, while the held-in breath seems bursting you asunder. You bear it for hardly a minute, but that minute lasts an age; and then--and then--no one can describe what follows. You are confused, and benumbed, and melting into nothing. I have gone through it.

"A ship I sailed in, when I was a young man, was run down one foggy night off the coast of Cuba. It was my watch on deck, and that is how I am here to tell the tale. The look-out gave no warning till we were close under the bow of a Spanish man-of-war bearing straight down on us. I shouted to port the helm. It was too late. The Spaniard was into us with a crash. He stove in our quarter, and sent us to the bottom. I was knocked down by the falling rigging, and found myself in the water, entangled among cordage, and drowning as I have described. I know nothing more--nothing till I found myself coming to, on board that foreign ship. The deathly sickness! The longing to sink back into unconsciousness! The dim dull misery and tingling in every limb! as the stagnant blood began once more to circulate. I hope you will never know them. It is bad to drown, but it is far, far worse to be brought to. It was days before I was myself again; but I had plenty of time to recruit. The ship was bound for the Philippines, and it was not till she reached Manilla that I was set ashore."

"Ah! then you have travelled, sir," said the Vice-Chancellor, scrutinising him with the condescension of a superior person recognising an interesting trait in an ordinary mortal. "Yet you have had time to make your fortune at home, and now you are embarking in politics, I hear. You deserve credit for the comprehensiveness of your energy, and will no doubt bring unusual information to bear on public affairs; but politics is as stormy a sea, and one more difficult to navigate than the one you know. It would be a pity, after weathering so many dangers, to make shipwreck there. We want good men in Parliament, but we want them on the right side."

"Is that the side of the patriots, Chancellor?--the men who went into office to save the country, and who made their own fortunes instead? The tide has turned, and left them high and dry on the bank, or in the offices they appointed themselves to fill."

It was a young man who spoke--fair-haired and broad-shouldered, with a complexion burnt to the colour of bricks by the exposure of outdoor life. His clothes were not new, but they fitted him, and there was that look of rest and balance in his limbs which leisure and exercise alone can give,--so different from the smug constraint with which life in chambers and offices stamps the man of affairs.

The Vice-Chancellor turned with the haughty stare of a schoolmaster on the urchin who has spoken out of turn. Colonel Carraway looked disgusted at the bad taste which could drag politics into social intercourse; and politics flavoured with personality as well, to judge by the thrill in the speaker's voice. Senator Deane rolled his cigar round to the other cheek, and--never mind, it is a dirty habit.

"Those Canadians," he observed to his neighbour, "get as hot over their politics as we do. 'What can there be to quarrel about in *their* small concerns?' say you? The same as in our big affairs--place and plunder, you may be sure. That's about all."

Joseph Naylor turned round to see who it was whose remark had brought the Chickenpip oration to a halt. "What! Walter Blount! You here! Where have you dropped from? The very last man I expected to see. And yet no one but you would have let his political zeal break out on so slight provocation. That comes of not being a native. You take the fever of politics the hotter for being new to it."

"But *you* are contesting our Riding just now."

"The more need to let alone for the present moment, so as to come fresh to the conflict. Party bickerings grow stale to the mind if one is always harping on them. Time enough to let out when I get back there. This is the seaside. But what brings *you* here?" resting his eyes admiringly on the other's sturdy limbs. "I see no sign of the relaxed system which is said to need bracing sea-air."

The young man did not change colour. The dusky vermilion of his sunburnt skin was incapable of a heightened tint; but he looked confused under the twinkling laughter of the other's eye. "I shall be selling out this Fall, so I thought I might run down here to the sea before moving West."

"West? Are you dreaming of making a fortune on the prairies?--turning farmer in earnest. Have you killed all the bears in your present neighbourhood, and exterminated the deer?"

"There will be neither bear nor deer within twenty miles before two years are over. The new railway runs right across my farm, and the speculators are prospecting all over the neighbourhood. I am offered a good price for my land. I shall sell, and go West somewhere, where settlers are fewer and game more abundant. No! prairie farming would not suit me. Even an improved farm in a good part of Ontario would be better than that; but I prefer the woods."

The circle round Naylor had now broken into groups occupied with their own talk, leaving him free to pursue his private gossip with his friend. He settled himself on a bench, buried his hands in his pockets, pushed out his feet in front, and blew a mighty cloud of smoke from his German pipe. "I declare I'm tired, Walter, with so much talking this morning. Now for a good old smoke! Where's your pipe?"

Walter sat down beside him and filled his pipe slowly and absently, as if his thoughts were on other things. Then he cleared his voice, lighted the pipe, and with as much off-handness as he could assume observed between the whiffs--

"Your family are with you, Mr Naylor?"

"My family is always with me. I carry the whole of it under my hat," he answered, looking his questioner straight in the eye, with a twinkle which plainly said, "Speak out if you have anything to say. I do not intend to help you."

The young man coughed. The smoke of his pipe had lost its way, and seemed trying for an outlet down his throat. "Mrs Naylor and her daughters are here, I understand?" he said at last.

"Yes."

There was a lengthened silence. "Yes" is not an answer to which the next observation can readily be attached. The questioner removed his pipe, and began nervously to examine what could be making it draw so badly; while the other watched him in silent amusement, tempered with a touch of good-natured pity.

"I wonder," Blount said at last, digging the charge carefully out of his pipe, and so making it unnecessary to raise his eyes to the other's face,--"I wonder what they will say to see me here?"

"Difficult to imagine," came the answer from the thickest of a bank of smoke.

"I fear I am not a favourite with Mrs Naylor."

"She told you not to call any more, I believe? That was pretty plain."

"Was it not too bad of her? What can she have against me? She has known me ever since I came to the country, and she used to be like a mother to me."

"That was imprudent. Now she sees it, I suppose. A mother of girls may become mother-in-*law* to some young fellow one day, and Mrs Naylor may feel that she ought to reserve herself for that. When girls leave school, you see, circumstances alter."

"I am sure I showed no unwillingness to take her for *my* mother-in-law."

"That was the trouble. She could have taken you for a son--a full son, understand--and you might have been brother to the girls, if that would have pleased you. But it didn't."

"How could it? Would it have satisfied you--to take a nice girl to picnics, and hold her shawl while another fellow danced with her?"

"Put it that way, and it does seem hard. But what is a mother to do? Her daughters' prospects ought to be her chief care."

"Do you think it is right to be mercenary, then? Is money to stand for everything? Is the fellow to count for nothing?"

"By no means! A good fellow it *must* be--a nice fellow and a gentleman if possible, or the girl's life is spoiled. No amount of money could make her happy with a ruffian or a cad. But you must remember that Mrs Naylor's girls are young yet, and I cannot blame her for wishing to look about before fixing their position for life."

"It is hard to be passed over merely for being the first comer. And they may happen on worse subjects as well as better."

"Quite true. There is a proverb about a girl who was so particular about the stick she went to cut, that she came to the end of the wood before she could make up her mind, and then she had to content herself with a crooked one, or go without. However, proverbial philosophy goes for nothing, you know; people like to try for themselves. Still, there is excuse for a mother wishing not to bury her accomplished daughter in the backwoods, as wife to a wild huntsman. One can understand that it would be pleasant for you, after being out all day with your gun and your dog, to find your dinner laid, and a pretty young wife beside a cosy fire waiting for you; but you cannot call it unreasonable if the lady's friends wish to secure her a less solitary home. When you are out, what will she have to amuse her but needle and thread? the chickens and the cows? You would not like to think of her sitting in the kitchen talking to the help; and yet you know they will be the only human creatures she will have to speak to when you are away."

"I told you I was selling out. She can choose her home anywhere between Gaspé and Vancouver."

"You would not like to live in a town, and a girl must have been bred on a farm to live happily on one afterwards."

"You leave the husband out of the calculation. Do you think she could be happy even in London or New York with a fellow she did not care for?"

"That is true; but she need not marry unless she cares."

"While even in the bush, if she liked the fellow, and he was fond of her, I think they might both be completely happy."

"I am with you there, my lad. Not a doubt of it,"--and he buried his hands deeper in his pockets, and bent his head forward to look at his boots, drawing a deep breath, and smoking harder than ever.

"Then why--Do you not think, Mr Naylor, you could bring your sister-in-law to see it in that light? You have always been a friend to me, since the first day I met you."

"Always your friend. Be sure of it. But I doubt my influence with Mrs Naylor; and, if I had any, I doubt if I ought to interfere. Girls cannot know their own minds till they have seen something of the world. They may mistake a passing fancy for real regard; and if they have married in the meantime, there are two lives spoiled, instead of one just a little scorched--and that only for the moment, perhaps," he added, after a pause. Then pulling himself together,-- "But what makes you talk like this to a crusty old bachelor? You cannot expect sympathy in your love-affairs from one who has resisted the illusions of sentiment as successfully as I have, surely?"

"I don't know. People are not bachelors and old maids for being harder than their neighbours, I suspect. I often fancy it is the other way. But at least you are not against my trying, are you? You will not do anything to make my chances less than they are already?"

"No, Blount; I'll do nothing against you. I could almost wish the girl took a fancy to you, for I believe you are real; and if she does, I will do nothing to dissuade her. Money and position are not everything, by any means."

CHAPTER VII.

A TABLEAU.

Mrs Deane and her party returned early from their drive. The loungers on the galleries saw them alight. They also saw Naylor come hurriedly forward, uncovered beneath the penetrating glare of noon, which singled out the scattered hairs of white among the brown about his temples, and made them glitter in a way not grateful to the feelings of a well-preserved bachelor in middle life--if he had but known it.

Why can a man not stick fast at five-and-thirty?--at least till he marries? He is at his best then physically, though mentally--if he has a mind worth mentioning--he may go on improving for another decade, if not longer. There is so much in life, and in one's self, worth knowing, and which is not found out till after the time when the knowledge would have been most precious has slidden by. The soul grows slower than the body, and may only be coming into bloom when those weariful crow-feet are beginning to gather round the eyes. But girls cannot be expected to see all this. How should they, when youth in themselves is held the crown and perfume of all their charm?

Still Naylor passed fairly well beneath the scrutiny of curious eyes--"the man who had been all but drowned that morning." He looked active, and even athletic, if somewhat gone to flesh. There was honesty in the steadfast grey eye, and modest self-possession in the fresh-coloured face. There was an earnestness, too, at the moment, which lent his bearing the dignity which is seldom attainable by the well-fed man of middle age and medium stature.

"Miss Hillyard," he said, "I have not had the happiness of being introduced to you; but surely, under the debt I owe you from this morning, you will allow me to offer you my grateful thanks."

"Mr Naylor," she answered, holding out her hand, "pray say nothing more about it. You have thanked me already, you know. But I am happy to make your acquaintance. I only did what any bather must have done who was near enough. I feel a little proud, I acknowledge, of my success, and pleased to have been of use; but do not talk of debts and gratitude: it sounds oppressive."

"I cannot take it so easily as that, Miss Hillyard. If you had not laid hold on me as you did, I should have gone under. I felt myself sinking when you touched me. I should have been down before Sefton reached me--I am sure of that. You saved my life: it is an obligation which I never can repay."

Rosa flushed a little, and looked down. There were a good many pair of female eyes in the gallery turned upon her, as she felt, with interest, and just a suspicion of envy, which could not but be gratifying. Still, it was embarrassing to stand out there on the gravel when the carriage had driven off, a cynosure for the eyes of all the people above; and just a trifle stagey, with this bareheaded gentleman presenting his acknowledgments with demonstrative respect. Queen Elizabeth would have liked it; but then, she was a public character: and besides, we prefer nowadays to keep our theatricals and our private life apart. At the same time, it was pleasant to hear this earnest and respectful gentleman assure her that she had saved his life: he looked so manly and so strong. It made her think well of herself to have been able to help him; and his clear grey eyes looked so truthful and brave in their level gaze, that she wondered how their parts in the morning's episode should have been so strangely reversed, and felt how safe she would have been in his company had the accident happened to herself.

As for him, standing before her and looking in her face, it seemed as if the years must have rolled back upon themselves,--the long savourless years since his youth,--the years which had been so bitter when first he had passed through his sore probation of sorrow; and then, when the lacerated spirit had learned to endure, had grown dull and insipid. He had felt himself alone, and that the joy of life was not for him; that others might love, but he must stand aside, an onlooker at the feast at which no place was laid for him. This new stirring in his benumbed emotions seemed like the summers he remembered long ago in the South, when the plants, made torpid by the arid heat, forget to grow, waiting through rainless weeks beneath a brazen sky. Then come the showers at last, and the roses put out buds and bloom anew, till winter comes to nip them.

He could not withdraw his eyes from the beautiful face before him. As he looked, it seemed transformed into another--another, yet still the same. This was more mature and strong; but that other might have been so too, if it had been given him to see it later. The soft brown eyes were the same, which lighted when she spoke, with the same blueness in the white, a lingering remainder from the freshness and purity of childhood. The hair was less dark than hers whom he remembered so well, and it had a crisper wave, which caught the falling sunbeams here and there, and flashed them brightly back like burnished bronze. There was rich warm colour, too, in the cheek, while that other had been pale; but the difference accorded with the change of scene between the bracing airs of the North and the thick hot languor of Louisiana. This face had vigour and maturity; the other had been more tender and more frail. Its charm had lain in a drooping softness claiming support, and promises for the future as yet unfulfilled; while this was in the glory of all her beauty, sufficient for herself in her supple strength--a companion for manhood, as the other had been the clinging cherished one for youth.

The silence had now lasted for nearly a minute. Rosa became uneasily aware that she was contributing a tableau for the entertainment of her fellow-guests, which might be interpreted as "Love at first sight," or a modern and burlesque rendering of "Pharaoh's daughter and the infant Moses," according to their several humours. She looked up in her companion's face, with rising colour in her own, and the flicker of a smile about her lips, while she held out her hand.

"You are staying here, Mr Naylor, are you not?" she said. "We shall see each other again. I am pleased to know you. Now I must follow Mrs Deane," and she turned and went up the stairs.

Naylor awoke from his reverie, and found himself alone. He felt how few and bald had been his expressions of obligation; and he had come forward prepared to deliver himself so fully, and in such carefully chosen words, when the near view of her face had raised long-buried recollections, and confused him with a sense of doubleness in the presence before him, and left his memory blank. The tender girl he had been parted from long ago, seemed associated and blended with the personality of this beautiful deliverer before him; and in an effort to disentangle the old impressions from the new, the precious moment for uttering his little speech had slipped away. Now he was alone, feeling how tongue-tied and thankless he must have appeared, and how impossible it would be to make another opportunity for delivering his speech.

And yet the speech might not be necessary now. She had received him very graciously, and had even said that she was pleased to know him--said it twice--and that they would meet again. "What more could he want?" he thought; "and was he not an ass to fancy that any set phrases of his could give pleasure to so glorious a creature?--and shabby at heart, to think that any string of words could lessen the obligation under which he stood? He must never forget the debt, or dream that by word or act it could be lessened; rather, he must treasure the recollection, and watch and be ready, if haply he might, some day, be privileged to serve or succour in return."

So thinking, he turned on his heel and went his way, leaving the spectators in the gallery to find some other object to divert their leisure.

CHAPTER VIII.

MRS WILKIE'S POWDER.

Rose left Naylor standing on the gravel, and went into the house, making her way leisurely up to her room.

The parlour door stood ajar, disclosing only darkness within, to eyes coming straight from the outer glare of sunshine. It seemed cool in there, with the rustling sea-breeze sifting fitfully through the closed Venetians; and there were gurglings of smothered laughter, which told that the place was not deserted. She stepped within the gloom, and, as her eyes grew used to it, she became able to make out the tenants.

A cheerful crew of girls, standing and seated in a ring, occupied the centre of the floor. In their midst sat old Mrs Wilkie on a low ottoman, which she occupied by herself, like a kind of throne, fanning herself industriously till the short grey curls upon her temples danced and fluttered in the artificial gale. The new blue ribbons in her cap and the old blue eyes in her head danced in unison and elation, and a proud self-satisfied smile played about her lips, and deepened the creases in her cheeks, which looked round and rosy like an overkept winter apple. She was in her glory, and she gave yet a more energetic flap to the palm-leaf fan, as she pursed her lips together, and prepared to speak again.

"Yes, my dears," were her words as Rose joined the circle, "blue was always my colour. You see I am fair--'like a lily,' the young men used to tell me I was," and she made a flourish with her fan. "But that was years ago," and she blew a sigh which made her chest heave like a portly bellows. "And then I had a colour--like a Cheeny-rose, the haverels would have it; but the Scotch gentlemen are great hands to blaw in the lugs of silly girls. Not that I was ever the wan to let my head be turned with their nonsense--but still they had grounds for what they said."

"You were a beauty," said Lettice Deane--"I can see that;" and the girls exchanged glances brimming with amusement and incredulity, such as those feel whose bloom is still in the present tense, when one of the have-beens puts in her claim to personal charms.

"Yes, my dear, I was admired--in my day," and the double chin went up with a snap, to join the rest of the self-complacent countenance.

"Don't say was, Mrs Wilkie," Lettice answered. "You are a dangerous woman still. It is well that mamma is with us here, to look after the old man, or--or-

--- Nobody knows what might happen. These old gentlemen are very susceptible."

"I don't think I am acquainted with your papaw, my dear," said the old woman, looking round the tittering circle with rising colour, and bridling as if the jest perhaps contained more truth than the scoffer wot of. "But I never was a flirt; and now, in my poseetion, one has to be careful, and set an example of propriety. But, as I was saying--and it's well for young people to know these things--you don't take proper care of yourselves in this country. You should see our Scotch complexions when we're young. Strawberries and crame--that's what we look like. But then we take a hantle care of our chairms; and we live healthy. It would be good for some Yankee girls if they were put through a course of proper conduck"--and she looked straight at Lucy Naylor, the most flagrant of the titterers--"and simple living, by one of our old Scotch grandmothers. You're for ever drinking icewater and hot tea, out here; and how can you expeck your insides to be healthy after that? And you're all the time at candies or pickles, not to speak of hot bread, and beef-steaks and pitaities for breakfast, as if ye had a day's ploughing before you-- and you just lounging on soffies and easy-chairs the whole forenoon, with some bit silly novel in your hands, and nothing to exercise either the body or the intelleck. My son, the Deputy Minister of Edication, says you're just destroying yourselves."

"Tell us about *him*, dear Mrs Wilkie," said Lettice, cutting short the prelection. "We know our faults already, though I fear we are not likely to mend them. Tell us about the young man. That will be far more interesting. What do you call his profession? Something very long-winded and grand, I know."

"He is the Deputy Minister of Edication, for the Province. And it *is* a grand poseetion for so young a man, or for any man--whatever you may think. And as for being 'long-winded,' you don't understand. He doesna preach, my dear--though he could do that too, if there was occasion. It was that I bred him to. But this pays better. He has his handsome income for just sitting still in his chair and seeing that his inferiors work hard enough. And then, there's what the opposeetion papers, with their ill-scrapet tongues, call pickin's! Oh yes! there's fine pickin's. But I mustna be telling tales out o' school."

"He must be a bishop, then, Mrs Wilkie, if he does not preach. We call boss ministers bishops. Do you call them deputies in Canada? How odd of you! And yet I danced with him last night. Think of dancing with a bishop! It sounds positively profane. What a country Canada must be!"

"The lassie's in a creel! My Peter's no that kind of minister avaw. I *bred* him for a minister, it's true--a minister of the Gospel, and very far from the same kind with your bishops, and their white gowns, and red things hanging down their backs. It's a U.P. he would have been, if I had had my way. But Peter preferred being a minister of the Crown; and there's no denying it *pays* better. There's no vows laid on a minister of the Crown. They may dance, or do anything they like--and very queer things some of them do like, it seems to me. But Mis-ter Wilkie's very circumspeck. He's Deputy Minister, you see. 'Deputy' means that all the pickin's"--and she winked, poor soul--"go to *him*; though sometimes he has to give a share to the chief--quietly, you understand, my dears, for the chief is responsible to Parliament, and there would be a scandal if it came out. They're fond of having a scandal in Canada when politics are dull. Then the chief has to resign, but the deputy just sits still. He's a servant of the Crown, you see; so he goes on drawing his pay just the same, whatever chief the politeetians may appint over him. That comes of our having a Crown in Canada. It's a fine institution, and troubles nobody. It would be telling you Yankees if you had wan. Ye wouldn't be turned out of your comfortable offices every four years, then; and more, it would keep you steady. Ye have no respeck and no reverence here, and no nothing;" and again she looked severely in Lucy Naylor's face--that ill-regulated young person having fallen a-laughing worse than ever.

"It must be nice to be married to a Deputy Minister of the Crown," Lettice observed, demurely.

"Ye may say that; and there's more than you thinks it, I can tell you, my dear. The young girls where we come from are just pulling caps to see who is to be the wan. It's really shameless the way they behave, and many's the good laugh me and Mis-ter Wilkie has at their ongoings."

"I suppose you are to choose the successful candidate?"

"A mother must know the kind that will suit her boay best. But it's a sore responsibeelity, my dears. It would be terrible if the expurriment didn't answer; and he's very hard to please, and terrible fond of his own way."

"Couldn't you say a good word for one of us here, dear Mrs Wilkie?" asked Lettice with her most winning smile. "Just see what a lot of us there are!--and we have all to find husbands yet: every variety of girl you can think of--tall and short, dark and fair. Surely one of us might answer. It would be a gain to all. If one were provided for, the chance would be better, by so much, for all the rest when the next *parti* came along."

"Peter must have intelleck, he says, and high culture. I'm fear'd ye wouldn't just answer, my dear--though you're a nice girl, I'll allow, and--well--and comely."

Lettice coloured to the temples, and her well-arched eyebrows contracted into something approaching to a frown. It is eminently provoking, when one fancies one has been rather successful in drawing out an oddity, and making sport, to find the tables suddenly turned, and one's self made the butt.

"I was not thinking of myself," she said, and there was a tremor of crossness in her voice, which made her discomfiture more amusingly evident to the rest--"or any one else, for that matter. I know I would not take a gift of the fellow, with his washy grey eyes, and stiff priggish pomposity."

"The grapes are sour, my dear. Did you never hear tell of the story of the fox? But never you mind. There's a man appinted for you, I make no doubt; and if there is, ye'll get him, for as long as he is about appearing."

There was a scream of laughter, and Lettice, too angry to trust her voice with a retort, turned on her heel and went out, while the old lady sniffed vindictively and pursed her lips, as if she could have said much more, had the offender allowed her time.

"The impident monkey!" she muttered at last. "Does she think she is to make sport of *me*, without getting as good as she gives?" "That's a forward girl," she added aloud. "It isn't becoming for a young woman to be putting in for a gentleman in that barefaced way. And ye needn't laugh, my dears; some of you are not much better. As for Mis-ter Wilkie, ye may keep your minds easy; he can get better than any of you where we come from, just for the raising of his finger."

"Poor Lettice!" said Rose. "Are you not a little hard on her? I am sure she did not mean to be provoking."

"If *you* say that, my dear, I am willing to suppose it. But really, I'm just bothered with young girrls trying to catch my son, every place I go. It's like the way bees come bizzing round a sugar-bowl; or wasps, I might say," and she flung an angry glance at Lucy Naylor, caught laughing again. "You are the young lady, if I'm not mistaken, that saved the man's life this morning? It was a noble ack; and you're an example to us women, that are more given to hang about a man till he sinks, than to bear him up when he's in trouble. You'll be staying here, like the rest of us?"

"Yes; I am here with Mrs Deane and her daughter."

"That girrl that was so impertinent to me just now?--pretending to cock her nose at a Deputy Minister! Set her up!"

"Miss Deane is an heiress and a beauty. All the men in Chicago were wild about her last winter. She did not mean to offend you, I am sure; though perhaps she is a little spoilt by all the attention she receives."

"An heiress, is she? And these will all be heiresses too, maybe? They're forward and saucy enough for that or anything," she added, tossing her head at the retiring figures trooping away to overtake Lettice, and leaving the old woman, whose good-humour they had worn out, standing alone with Rose. "If it was you, now, I would be proud to hear that ye were an heiress, and to know you. Ye've got spurrit; and I'm sure ye have sense as well as good looks. Ye're not so young as thae light-headed tawpies, with their empty laughs, that have gone out just now, but you're just in your prime."

"I am five-and-twenty," said Rose, with a twinkle of dawning mischief.

"That's within two years of the age I was myself when I was married. It would be just one like you that I could welcome to my bosom, for a daughter," and she looked graciously in the other's face, to accept the answering look of gratitude which she felt was her due. "It's a sore responsibeelity, I can tell you, to a right-thinking mother, to get her only son--and *such* a son!--properly settled in life. They've no sense, even the best of men, when it comes to choosing a wife. There's a glamour comes over them, and they just fall a prey to some designing cuttie that has nothing but the duds she stands in, and neither sense nor experience. But I mean to stand between my boay and that misfortune, at any rate."

"He must feel deeply indebted to you."

"I don't know if he does, my dear. The men are contrar' cattle, and very thrawn. But I have my duty to do. He's my objeck in life. I left home to come out and live with him in a foreign land; and that was no small sacrifice at my time of life, I can tell you. It's true he has a fine piseetion and a good income; but if ye had seen the way he was being put upon, and the waste, when I came out to look after him, it would have made your hair stand up. A whole peck of pitaities biled every day for wan man's dinner! The cook's mother kept pigs, ye see. That's where the pitaities went. But I made a cleen sweep, I can tell you."

"It must have been rather trying to you."

"Eh yes! it's been very hard upon my nerves. I'm not strong; though perhaps ye wouldn't think it. My colour's so good that nobody will believe there's much the matter with me. But my heart's affecket, my dear. If you could just feel the palpitations--thump--thump--like a smiddie hammer! ever since thae girrls with their jawing went out,"--and she laid her hand upon her ample chest and closed her eyes.

"How distressing! Does your medical man give you hopes of getting over it?"

"That's in Higher Hands, my dear. We are trying the effecks of sea-air on my complaint, just now. That's what has brought us all the way down from Ontario. The doctor thinks I want bracing, and he gives me poothers to take. You see, it's homoeopathy we are trying. And that 'minds me: this is my time for a poother. What can have come over Peter that he isn't here to give me it?"

"Can you not take your powder yourself?"

"No; it's small and delicate, and not easy to apply. The doctor ordered it to be sprinkled on the tongue. I wish Peter was here. The thoughtless rascal!"

"On the tongue? How odd! Do you think I could do it for you?"

"My dear, if you would! Ye're a dear lamb, and ye'll be a treasure to any mother-in-law that gets you."

"Have you the powder?"

"I carry them about with me, to prevent accidents, when I'm living in a strange house. The maids might be for tasting them, ye see, and nobody knows what might happen."

Mrs Wilkie sat down in a chair facing the window, handed a tiny parcel to Rose, and stretched out her feet in front, while she laid back her head, grasping the chair-arms, shutting her eyes tight, and opening her mouth wide to display the flat red tongue. It was a moment of tension with her; she was stretched to her utmost, holding her breath, and with every muscle tightened in expectant rigidity.

Rose opened the parcel, which contained a pinch of white powder, and proceeded to administer; but the appearance of the patient was so comic that she had to forbear while calming her risible inclinations, lest her hand should shake and the precious remedy fall on a wrong place. At length she felt steady, and began to sprinkle as directed. But the sprinkling took time. The powder was to be evenly scattered over the member, or evil results would ensue; and meanwhile the patient was holding in her breath. She clutched the chair-arms, and strove valiantly; but nature gave way at length. Just as the last flake descended to its place, the imprisoned wind broke loose with a mighty sigh; a white cloud ascended between herself and Rose, while the outstretched jaws relaxed and came together; she opened her eyes and sat up, but the "poother" was scattered on the viewless air, and the old lady had little homoeopathy that morning.

CHAPTER IX.

BETWEEN FRIENDS.

There is considerable monotony in seaside life, but it is monotony of a different kind from the everyday existence of the rest of the year; and in this complete change its principal charm and benefit consist. The home-life of a number of households is laid aside for the time, and the heterogeneous elements are thrown for the moment into a larger whole, forming an unstable compound--a salad of humanity where the sweets, the sours, and the bitters find themselves in new combinations with one another, and united for the time in a *sauce piquante* of fresh air and idleness. There can be no great variety in the occupations; picnics, excursions, drives, rides, walks, form an ever-recurring ditto, to which the unaccustomedness alone gives flavour.

There is rest for the workers, and society for the home-keeping, but genuine delight only for the very young, whose gregarious instincts are still unblunted, and who find in the presence of one another the exhilaration of spreading their callow wings in early flights.

For the mother-birds, however, there is anxiety. In this larger poultry-yard their chicks grow wilder than they have ever known them before. The broods get mixed, and wander into undreamt-of mischief, pullets consorting with cockerels of another breed, chickens with ducklings venturing into the water, while Dame Partlet clucks and flutters about, pecking and distracted.

Mrs Naylor sat fidgeting and restless among the matrons who presided over and superintended the enjoyments of their youthful charges. Lucy was causing her anxiety. "Who was that tall man she was dancing with?--dancing not for the first time or the second, but the third time without a break. And how unnecessarily intimate they appeared! Could she not fan herself if she felt warm, when they stopped for breath?--instead of letting an awkward stranger raise tempests which were blowing her hair into unsightly confusion, and making her so needlessly conspicuous." If a gentleman was warranted "nice," she did not object to his paying attention to her girls, but she wanted assurance of the niceness. She leant over to the nearest neighbour who seemed at leisure to answer her inquiries, and with whom, being a stranger, she would not compromise herself, whatever might be said.

The neighbour was Miss Maida Springer, a damsel scarcely any longer young, seeing her thirtieth birthday would be her next, who hovered on the confines of the dance, and looked hungrily after young men leading other maidens out, and wondering why no one came for her. She sat under the wing of an elder as lonely as herself--the widow Denwiddie, who varied the sober tenor of her life by spending a fortnight each summer among the gaieties and dissipations by the sea. She was bidding the widow observe things curious in the whirling crowd of dancers as they passed.

"See that great thing in pink," she had said last. "Positively stout. And what a colour for a large woman to wear! If it had been black, now, or blue, or even white----" and she glanced down approvingly at her own blue and white washed muslin. "Just watch the slow revolving heap. Ain't she like an iceberg out at sea, growing pink in the setting sun? And her poor little bit of a partner, racing to get round her on time! My! mustn't he feel warm! He reminds me of an ant trying to carry home a seed of wheat. Why don't he choose a slim one like himself?" and she ran her eye down her own spare form, which was certainly as slim as the absence of superfluous tissue could make it, with spider-like arms and wrists which would not be kept out of sight,--thinking how much freer the gentleman would have felt in the clasp of these slender tendrils.

"Look at that one's feet. Well, I never! What a size! I wonder how she can venture to stand up and dance. Ain't it good for the beetles they ain't none of them here?" and then, by a strange coincidence, a pair of number-one shoes stole out in front to show themselves--things small and narrow, on which it seemed wonderful that a human being could stand. But then a few bones can be packed away in very little room.

"Will you kindly tell me," asked Mrs Naylor, "who is that gentleman by the wall, with a lady's fan in his hand?--the one with the limp hair, brushed up so strangely above his forehead."

"The tall fine man with drab hair? That's Mr Aurelius Sefton of Pugwash--one of the most rising pork-packers in the whole West, they do say."

"Pugwash? What a name! And pork! That accounts for the sleekness of his hair. Lard--depend upon it."

"You think the lard has got in his hair? Well, now, ain't you droll! Perhaps it has. But if lard has got in the hair, they do tell there has money got in the pocket. Do you lumber folks in Canady, now, have chips in your hair--chips and sawdust?"

Mrs Naylor looked dignified, and turned away. The magnates of her country deal in lumber. It is quite a high-class pursuit, and not to be spoken of in the same breath with pork--a horrid butcherly business, in which no person of refinement would condescend to make his fortune.

Maida raised her eyebrows, and turned to her friend.

"Ain't we high-strung, just! we aristocrats from Canady? What difference can it make whether it's hogs or logs a man makes his pile by, so long as he makes it? And I guess, if there's been less money made in pork, there's been a sight more lost in lumber. I had a friend once----" and she coloured faintly, looking down, and heaving a sigh so demonstrative that her friend turned and looked at her.

"Yes, my dear?" said the widow, with a droop in her voice in token of sympathy. "You *had* a friend? That sounds sad. Whaar did he go to?"

"He went away; and that's why it always seems as if something was catching my breath and making me feel low, whenever lumber is spoken of. *He* went to Canady in the lumbering interest, because prospects were better there than in old Vermont. He promised to come back when he had made his pile, and I promised to wait. It's nothing so mighty unusual for young folks to do; and it's real feelin' of you to shake your head and look at me like that, Mrs Denwiddie. But don't let folks see you a-doing it; they might wonder."

"Ah yes!" heaved the widow, in deep sympathy; "I can understand. It's the tender way us trustin' women always has. We never tell our love, but just let folks think it's a big caterpillar has got in the heart of the cabbage, so to speak; or rather, I should say, liver and dispepsy that's eatin' our young looks away. It's disappinted love, now--is it, my dear--that's wearin' you to a shaddy? I know the feelin' well," and another sigh undulated her portly figure. "It's twenty years, come Fall, since I was left a lone woman, and hope has been tellin' me flatterin' tales ever since; but the men are that backward--they just look foolish when I shake their hands friendly-like and invite them to sit a bit, after seein' me home from evenin' meetin'; and away they go, sayin' never a word, and leavin' me with no more appetite for supper than if I'd eaten it a'ready."

"Do you mean that you would marry again?"

"I would then--and don't you forget it--if ever I get the chance."

Maida glanced sidewise, and shrank the least bit possible away.

"You think me light-minded now, maybe, my dear? I don't wonder at it. Them as hain't been married don't know how lonesome it feels to see just the one cup and saucer laid out beside the teapot at mealtimes."

"There must be memories. It would be sweet, I should have thought, to dwell on the idea that one had gone before, and was waiting across the river to be joined by the old companion."

"Oh yes; that's sweet--in a way. At least it was, when it was a dear young minister that was sayin' beautiful things about the Golden Shore, and comfortin' the bereaved. But twenty years is a long time. The Rev. Mr Beulah is a married man now, with a fine young family of his own. Folks have forgotten about my affliction this many a year. And as for Hezekiah----I don't hold with them spiritualists. He's more to do, you bet, than to be coming around frightenin' a lone woman with messages rapped out on a tea-table, or to mind whether I'm married or single. I'll be laid beside him when the time comes; that's as it should be. But it would be real pleasant to have some one for company in the meantime. It's a vale of tears--we've Gospel for that; but if ever you come to my time of life, you'll be wishin', like me, you had some one to dry your eyes in it."

Maida sighed disappointedly. Her friend's sentiments were too robust for the plaintive tone in which that word "lumber" had been tempting her to indulge. Mrs Denwiddie, on the other hand, felt talkative, and there being no one else whom she could address, she accommodated herself to her friend's mood.

"Is it long, now, since you saw him last?--your friend, I mean."

"He went ten years ago."

"Ten years! That's half a lifetime. Have you been gettin' letters from him for ten years?"

"He used to write--at first, that is. Then he would send a newspaper. Now, I don't know where he is, or what he is doing. I wish I did. All would be forgiven and forgotten, if he only would return."

"It's real good of you to speak like that, my dear. It takes a woman to be true and forgivin' like that. I wonder what the young man will be doin', now, all this time?"

"He is trying hard to make that weary fortune, to be sure. He is ambitious."

"And he don't allow himself even the encouragement of writin' to tell you how he's gettin' on. Do you think there could be some one up there encouragin' him?"

"Mrs Denwiddie!"

"There's no tellin', my dear, what the men are up to. They ain't faithful and endurin' like us."

"I have waited. I can wait."

"It does you credit, my dear. But a girl's youth won't wait. How about settlin' yourself in life?"

Maida tightened her lips. She knew all that as well as Mrs Denwiddie; but what right had the woman to inspect her life in this fashion? to pull open the fold in which she chose to hide her inner self, and pry and probe in wanton curiosity?--the merciless and contemptuous curiosity with which married women will card out and examine the tangled threads of a spinster's being. She knew well enough the hopelessness of what, for want of another name, she thought of as her "attachment." Yet why could it not be taken at such small worth as she put upon it? She had not boasted of it. She knew its little value too well. But it was all she had, and why might she not wear it, having nothing else? That evening she was sitting a wallflower while the rest were merry--with no one to lead her out or make her a sharer in the gaiety. What wonder if she should wish to refer to a deferred engagement, and furbish up the poor little relic of a might-have-been, the one bit of romance she ever had, if only to seem less forlorn in her own eyes? And this old thing by her side, as lonely and shut out from the revelry as herself, and who, but for her, would have sat absolutely solitary--that *she* should take upon her to be inquisitive and unpleasant! It was intolerable. She gathered her spare skirts more tightly round her, and edged some inches away upon the haircloth sofa she divided with her "friend." She would have risen altogether, but where was she to go? To what other companion could she join herself? She was not intimate with any of the other guests, married or single, old or young. She belonged, poor soul, to the order of bats--both bird and quadruped, yet accepted by neither. In the marrying aspect, she was regarded as altogether out of the running, while old and young agreed each in classing her with the other variety--too old to be a girl, not old enough to be a tabby--and nobody minded her when other company could be got. She felt it all, though she bravely ignored and struggled with her fate, living through many a tragic pang which no one ever suspected. She dared not put her position to the test by quarrelling with the widow. Already she saw herself flitting in and out among the revellers, unheeded, like a disembodied spirit. Where she sat she had at least a companion, and was safe from pity. She choked back her anger as a luxury she could not afford, and was ready to respond when Mrs Denwiddie, warned by symptoms that she might be left solitary in the crowd, realised that she must have been disagreeable, and set herself to open a new conversation in a less personal strain.

How many of us would dispense with our dear friends, if we were only sure we could get on without them!

CHAPTER X.

A MOTHER'S CARES.

Mrs Naylor went back to her chair to digest the information she had received. Pork and Pugwash were not ideas attractive to her refined imagination; but if there was money! The sons of "first families" in the East were sent West at times, she knew. Why not to Pugwash as well as other places? If Mr Aurelius Sefton were indeed well off, even Pugwash might be an endurable place to live in. Millinery is sent from New York by express all over the country, and railways have brought Everywhere within reach of civilisation. "Yes; if the man had his hair cut, and his manners chastened down by a judicious mother-in-law, he really was not ill-looking. She would find out brother Joseph, and bid him have an eye on the man, and try what he could find out about him from the other people in the house. It did seem, to see the pair still circling cheerfully together, as if something might be brought to pass, if that were desirable. Yet, if it were not, she must see that the girl did not compromise herself, and get classed with the easily accessible." "Ah!" she said to herself, "the anxieties of a fond mother! How are my poor nerves to stand the strain of settling those two girls?" She realised how good she was, feeling strengthened thereby, and almost heroic, as she rose and moved slowly round the outskirts of the dance in search of her brother-in-law.

The company was more numerous than usual that evening. A brass band from Lippenstock stood on the verandah, and brayed waltzes in through the open windows; and three or four omnibus-loads of strangers from Blue Fish Creek, some miles along the shore, had arrived to assist. The rooms were full, and it was not easy to pick out any one in the crowd. She made her way from doorway to doorway and past the windows, outside which the men not actively engaged were wont to lounge; but no Joseph could she see--though it was in such situations that he generally stood watching the gambols he no longer cared to join. She walked along the neighbouring galleries; but these seemed taken possession of by dancers cooling off, and sauntering in the moonlight till they were ready for another start.

At last, in the shadow of a pillar and leaning on the balustrade, she came upon a pair looking out seaward, in intimate talk. She thought she recognised something in the gentleman's back, and figure, and close-cropped hair. She almost fancied she knew him; yet who could he be? The lady wore a dress less simple than the attire of the other girls that evening. There was a shimmer of satin here and there among the dimness of thinner fabric--

"Like glints of moonshine in a clouded sky"--

and the suggestion of pale yellow, with a bunch of crimson on the shoulder, where it reached beyond the shadow which fell on the rest of the figure.

Mrs Naylor was a woman; and while she might not be able to recall the back of her own father, a gown once seen was imprinted on her memory, and she recognised it at once. "Miss Hillyard," she said to herself, "the heroine--in her lovely Paris dress. I wonder whom she has got there. That is not the contradictious Scotch schoolmaster, at any rate, with his awkward knees and elbows. The men seem wild about her. Natural, that, in the men. But a little unfeminine," she could not help thinking, "in a lady to swim so well. And it would have been in better taste if she had dressed more quietly for this once, after making herself so remarkable in the morning. But then she is a Yankee, and perhaps not altogether a lady. One never knows how to class those people. Best let them alone;" and her thoughts reverted to Mr Sefton of Pugwash, and she felt much inclined to return to the ball-room and get Lucy away from him without further seeking enlightenment.

At that moment the gentleman in shadow began to speak more loudly, pointing to where the moonlight made a patch of flickering lustre on the hazy sea.

"How bright the moonlight lies out yonder on the water! Every ripple catches it a moment and throws it back, till the surface seems to burn.... How different it was this morning! How different it must be down deep below, and how easily I might be there now--cold and stiff, rolling amongst the sea-weed, and slime, and things nibbling in the darkness! It is a horrible reflection, and it would have come true if it had not been for you."

The lady demurred, and moved, and asked if they had not better go in now; and Mrs Naylor beheld her brother-in-law turn round and lead his companion back among the dancers.

She could scarcely believe her eyes. Joseph was forty-seven. She knew the date of his birth. He had never cared to dance within her recollection, and she had known him almost since her marriage. She remembered his coming home from sea about that time, a sad-eyed youth, who avoided company, and lived in a sort of patient gloom, finding his sole distraction in close application to business. Her husband whispered that he had met with a disappointment into which they must not pry, but rather strive by unspoken sympathy and kindness to reconcile him to his lot, and wean him from his sorrow.

In time the cloud upon his spirits had seemed to lift. He was too kind-hearted not to take interest in the people among whom he lived; and, sympathising with them in their joys, his own depression by degrees was lightened. A man's capacity, even for suffering, is limited. Divide his attention, and you mitigate the intensity of his woes. It is the self-centred egotist whose troubles kill him, or may drive him mad, because he is incapable of distraction. To Joseph the better part of his life had seemed over, and work his only remaining resource. Yet he had never closed his heart against the cares and pleasures of his fellows, and he felt a wholesome interest in all that went on around him, like a father watching the opening hopes of children, who have not learnt to misgive, or dread the nipping frosts of disappointment.

His sister-in-law, not being addicted to moral analysis, probably did not consider this; but she had seen his despondency clear away, and knew that he was the kindest, most cheerful, and most popular man she had ever met--ready to join in every pastime, and differing from the rest only in a premature middle-aged benevolence, setting in before he was thirty, which found pleasure in amusing others, without seeking anything for himself. He had seemed impervious to female charms through all the years she had known him, and especially he had avoided dances--or if by chance he found himself at one, only joining when charity led him to the side of some neglected wallflower. And here he was to-night, when there was no benevolent occasion for it whatever, leading out the best-dressed woman in the room, with an ardour which would have seemed more natural in him twenty years before. True, the lady had saved his life; but it seemed a droll way of manifesting gratitude to *dance* with her, at his age. Her eyebrows made a satirical twitch upwards, and she sighed impatiently at men's lack of common-sense. The present was no time to unburden her anxieties--that was plain; and meanwhile she would saunter round the crowd, and watch him in his new character of middle-aged youngster.

The evening was warm, but in the dancing-room it was positively hot. The atmosphere quivered with the blare of sounding brass, and the whirling figures, chasing the fleeting strains, raised a sirocco of sultry air and dust. Still the young people seemed to like it, and Mrs Naylor looked on in wonder, forgetting that she had once been young herself. But who were those in the farthest corner, keeping themselves so well clear of the hurrying hubbub?--revolving dreamily on the outer edge, in perfect sympathy and time, and in an orbit of their own--avoiding collision with the meteors and comets of the greater system, spinning calmly and smoothly on the flood of sound, engrossed with themselves, and indifferent to all the world beside.

She looked again. The girl was her own daughter Margaret; but who was the man in whose arms she was so restfully and intimately revolving? Her self-reliant daughter was not wont to dance in that clinging fashion, and she could not imagine what dweller at Clam Beach could have won her to such unaccustomed softness. What masterful bird could so have won upon the fancy of her favourite chick? Was he one of the proper sort? But Margaret was too high-spirited to take up with a cross-breed, and she felt less solicitous than had it been that featherhead Lucy. Still she was curious to know who could have tamed proud Meg to so mild a demeanour. It was not young Petty. She could have wished that it had been. This one was not so tall, neither was he raw-looking, as--candour compelled the admission--was Mr Walter Petty--just a little; but then he was young yet, and it would soon wear off, with his prospects and assured position. This one was thoroughly in possession of himself and all his limbs. How deftly he steered and threaded their way, without stop or collision, among the less skilful dancers! How strong he looked, and calm, without heaviness! She could have wished herself young again, to be danced with by a partner such as he. In their continuous whirling, and the perpetual intervening of other couples, she could not make out or recognise his face. After a while they stopped, and she moved from where she had been standing, to get a better view. How intimately Margaret stood up to him and talked, with her flapping fan interposed between them and the rest of the world!

Mrs Naylor's curiosity increased, and she drew nearer. "What!" she almost cried out aloud. "Walter Blount! How comes he here? This must not be!" And flushing, and tightening her lips, she walked across to where they stood. To think that after all the management she had expended in making her brother-in-law bring them to the seaside, and so remove her girl for a while beyond the reach of the "detrimental" whose fascinations threatened to ruin her prospects, the aggravating youth should have followed them! It was too provoking. She sniffed indignantly, and bore down on the offenders, tightening her lace shawl about her shoulders, and looking tall and stately with all her might.

"Margaret, my dear," she said, "you are dancing a great deal too much. You will be knocked up to-morrow, and I mean you to accompany me to Boston."

Margaret was taken aback. Her mother's habitual seat was in the conversation-room, at the other end of the suite, with two pairs of folding-doors and all the dancers between. It was to avoid her observation that they had been confining their career to this far-off corner, and her sweeping thus down on them was altogether unexpected. She let go her partner's arm, and with drooping eye and pouting lip prepared to follow her mother, like a naughty child detected in the act.

"Mrs Naylor," said Blount, "will you not speak to me?"

"How d'ye do, Mr Blount? I was not aware you were at Clam Beach."

"It used to be 'Walter,' and you allowed me to call you aunt. Why this change?"

"That was nonsense. We are not related. You are not a stripling now, Mr Blount, and my daughters have grown to be young women since then."

"That does not make me feel the less regard for you and them, dear Mrs Naylor. It is not our fault that we grow older."

"Why have you left your farm? These haunts of idleness and dissipation are no good place for a young man who should be making his fortune. Your stock will be straying and breaking down fences; and how is your harvest-work to go on in your absence? I am sure your friends would not approve if they knew."

"I have sold the farm--sold it very well--and I shall soon be looking out for another."

"I am sorry to hear you are becoming unsettled. Roving from place to place is the sure way for a young man to ruin himself. Remember the proverb about rolling stones.... Now, Margaret, if you are ready we will go." And drawing her daughter's arm through her own, she sailed away, leaving Blount disconsolate.

"I am amazed, Margaret, at your want of common-sense and proper feeling," she began, as she led the captive back by the gallery towards the place where she was wont to sit. But she got no further with her harangue. Mr Peter Wilkie, coming through a window, intercepted her retreat, requesting Margaret for the favour of a dance.

Margaret was declining with thanks, being in no mood for further exercise; but her mother, whose brow had cleared at once on the new-comer's appearance, interposed.

"Indeed, Margaret, I think a dance would do you good. What an oppressive evening, Mr Wilkie! We came out here for a breath of coolness, but I do think it is better for young people not to yield. The more you give way to the heat, Margaret, my dear, the limper you will become. A dance with a good partner is far the best way of throwing off the oppression."

Margaret felt a little doubtful about the goodness of the partner, but she said nothing, and took Mr Peter's arm without further demur. What did it matter? Her evening was irretrievably spoilt. Besides, her mother meant to be disagreeable--that was abundantly plain--and she had better accept the offered deliverance. She accompanied Peter back into the room. She laid her hand on his shoulder and they began to dance.

If there is no method of motion more perfect than a good waltz, there is no purgatory so grievous as a bad one. Racing, stumbling, jolting, and running into other couples, with the danger of getting entangled among the feet and knees of her partner at every stride, and her ear outraged by his disregard of the music, Margaret could only liken their progress to a hurdle-race at a country fair, as they broke through the bars of the music, or cleared them helter-skelter. At length she was able to stop, and Mr Peter, somewhat giddy, and holding on till his head grew steady, drew a long breath.

"Heh! that was fine! The best dance I've had to-night. You and me suit one another splendid, Miss Margaret. Let's have another turn. Are you ready?"

"Really, Mr Wilkie, you must let me rest a moment, I am quite out of breath;" and she fanned herself industriously, taking care, however, not to include the partner this time. "How oppressive it is here! Do you not think a breath of fresh air on the gallery would be pleasant?" and Mr Wilkie, without at all intending it, found himself promenading in the moonlight, when he would rather have been regaling the company with his antics in the dance. Like other rugged and ungraceful men, he had a high opinion of his personal graces; and his doting mother, who worshipped his very shadow, had conspired with his natural vanity to breed a self-admiration which tempted him in expansive moments to display himself before an admiring world. He would have liked to exhibit under the lights in the crowded ball-room, with this fine girl hung gracefully on his shoulder, as he knew she could pose herself; but if that was not to be, at least she was a young person of intelligence who could appreciate a man of talent. He resigned himself to the comparative seclusion, stroked his chin, and cleared his voice, preparatory to saying something smart.

What the observation was to have been, nobody knows. It is in Limbo with other good things which have missed their opportunity. It was Margaret who spoke--

"Mr Blount! You out here! Found it too warm inside? So did we. How pleasant it is here!"

At that moment the music ceased. The dance was ended, and Mr Peter Wilkie, his smart saying unsaid, found himself exchanging a valedictory smile with his companion, who somehow had become detached from him, and, before he well understood the situation, was wafting away with Mr Blount, leaving him alone with his handsome shadow in the moonlight.

CHAPTER XI.

DISCUSSING A SUITOR.

Is there some connection between a maiden's tresses and the workings of her mind? When the braids are coiled in shining order for the captivation of the world, are her thoughts as well confined in conventional rolls and waves conforming to the fashion of the time? Poets love to dwell upon her "locks": can it be because they guard her confidences that they have named them so? There is more in this than a mere wretched pun; there is a connection between sound and sense--involuntary, no doubt, but the beginnings of language are all involuntary. When the hair is unbound, the mind is freed from the trammels of convention and reserve; and this may be why, at hair-brushing time, as I have heard, girls' tongues are wont to wag so freely.

There must be infinite relief to the poor little head, and brain benumbed, when the weight of firmly drawn and twisted hair is unbuckled and let down, and a refreshing stimulation of thought in the action of brush and comb, spreading and airing and drawing out the uncomfortable glory.

Margaret and Lucy Naylor had retired for the night, but not as yet to rest. Relieved from hair-pins, they stood before their glasses in freedom and disarray, more charming far than when decked out to meet the public eye, which might not, alas! be privileged to behold them now.

Yet doubtless there is a happiness in being handsome, for its own sake, even if one is alone. One may legitimately rejoice in beauty though it be one's own; and it were churlish to libel that as vanity which is common to all things beautiful. See how the roses spread their petals to the light, and how birds of starry plumage perch in solitary places in the sun, to preen their feathers and display their brilliant dyes!

The girls were pretty seen at any time, but when busied in these secret mysteries they were vastly more so. The glossy abundance hung down like mantles over the pearly shoulders and far below their waists, and the supple white arms held up and played among the falling waves of hair, which flashed like skeins of pale and ruddy gold-thread in the flicker of the candles. The glittering veil half hid their smiling features, but ever and anon the eyes flashed out beneath the shadow, more brightly than their wont, answering to lips of red, and rows of small white teeth, and gurgling rounds of laughter.

The doings of the evening were all gone over again, the successes won anew; and in relation, what had seemed but trifling incidents at the time, grew bigger, and under merry comment vastly entertaining. Lucy had most to say. She was the chatterbox, and had much to tell about the gentlemen she had danced with, and their sometimes rather vapid talk. Could those lordly wiseacres have heard the *résumé* and description of their stiff-backed endeavours to converse and please, they would have been surprised, and some of them not over-gratified, at the shrewd commentaries of the pretty, timid, and not too clever little thing they had trifled with so condescendingly.

Margaret had much less to say, but she was in equally good spirits. It was with a very old friend that she had mostly been passing the time, so there was nothing to tell, though Lucy looked a little incredulous when she said as much; but her evening had been none the less pleasant on that account, to judge from her ready appreciation of her sister's fun.

There was a knock while the talk was at its briskest, but in the babblement and laughter it was not heard. The knock was repeated, and this time the speaker stopped short in the middle of a sentence, and both turned round and looked at each other.

"It is mamma," whispered Lucy.

Margaret's countenance fell; she even frowned a little. Something unpleasant was going to happen, she felt sure.

"Let's blow out the lights and jump into bed," suggested Lucy.

"No use," said Margaret. "Open the door and get it over as quickly as possible. I shan't say a word, and she will run herself out of breath the sooner."

"Nonsense!" and Lucy blew out one of the candles as she spoke. "She will forget about it in the morning if we fall asleep now. I don't want to have the feeling of a well-spent day spoilt by a lecture."

The knock was repeated more peremptorily than before. It was too late to pretend unconsciousness now. Margaret went sullenly to the door and admitted her mother.

"What an uproar you two girls are making in here--din enough for a dozen--chattering like magpies, and laughing at this hour of the night, when decent people are in their beds! Nice complaints and remarks the people in adjoining rooms will make to-morrow!--though they may not venture to speak to *me* about it," she added grandly, as if she dared any one to take that liberty. "But that makes it worse. We cannot explain or set them right when they tattle behind our backs, and the stories will grow bigger and worse, till no one knows what they may come to.... You thoughtless pair! Lucy there speaking at the very tip of her voice. It will be a wonder if the people through the partitions do not know every word she has been saying--something, most likely, which will do her no credit. Mrs Chickenpip, I may tell you, is your neighbour on that side, and she does not spare people who annoy her. For your own sakes you had better respect her slumbers. She passed when I was hammering at your door, and she looked many things at me which good manners prevent people from saying; but she will find an opportunity of expressing them to some one else, or I am mistaken."

"Tiresome old cat," said Lucy. "No one will mind her. She is too grim and proper. Nobody heeds what childless old women say about young people."

"Old women? She is younger than I am. Would you speak of your own mother----?"

"Oh no, mammy dear! Nobody thinks of its own pretty mamma in that way;" and she threw her arms round her mother's neck.

"Have done, Lucy! I am in no mood for fooling, I assure you. Let me alone, and be quiet. It was you, Margaret, that I wanted to talk to. We must come to an understanding at once. This kind of thing which has been going on down-stairs must come to an end. I have been inexpressibly shocked and pained. It is more than my poor health can stand. Would you bring my hair with sorrow to the grave?" ... "Grey hairs with sorrow to the grave," was the Scriptural quotation which had come into her mind; but even to make a rhetorical point, she felt that she could not afford to attribute greyness to her carefully tended braids. She put up her hand and stroked them tenderly, which disturbed the thread of her argument, and she came to a stop, with her eyes resting reproachfully on her elder daughter.

Margaret was aware that she had better let the lecture run itself down. Interruptions, she knew by experience, acted like winding up a clock, and set it off again, tick-tack, on a refreshed career. She bore the reproachful gaze in silence as long as she was able, but at last it grew too much for her, and rather sullenly she answered--

"What do you mean, mother?"

"You know very well what I mean. Have I not told you many times that that childish nonsense with young Blount must be given up?"

"Is it our engagement you mean?" Margaret answered, with heightened colour. She knew that she was unwise to speak, but her temper was rising. It always *would* rise, she knew not how, when her mother spoke of "young Blount."

"Your what?" her mother cried, indignantly. "I will not hear of such a thing. I have forbidden you to be engaged to him. You shan't be engaged to him; and now that you force me to it, I forbid you to speak to him. An abominable young man!--worming himself deceitfully into families where he is not wanted. Was there ever anything so ungentlemanlike as his sneaking down here after us, although he had been as good as forbidden the house at home?

He had not the candour to come to me and say, 'Mrs Naylor, I am here;' but slyly waylays you in a crowded ball-room, to hold surreptitious interviews. I never heard of anything so atrocious in my life. I could not have believed it. But it rewards me for my imprudence in taking up a stranger, merely to oblige your uncle Joseph, and being kind to him--warming a viper in my bosom, that he might turn and sting me!"

This was fine, and Mrs Naylor stopped for breath.

"You have no right to say such things, mother," Margaret answered, hotly. "Walter never was ungentlemanlike. He could not be, if he were to try. And he is no sneak. He is as brave and honest as the day; and I have heard you say as much yourself, formerly, when he used to visit us. You often said he was the nicest young man of your acquaintance."

"And this is the reward of my ill-judged hospitality--having him come to me with your uncle, when you were both children! I see my imprudence now; but at least my daughter might spare me," and Mrs Naylor put her handkerchief to her eyes. "That a mother's solicitude should be taunted thus, by the very child she is trying to shield from the effects of her injudicious good-nature! Oh, Margaret, you are cruel!"

Margaret felt shocked with herself. To think that she should bring tears to her mother's eyes! How hard and obdurate she must surely be! She had never felt so wicked in all her life before. Yet how to mend it? She would gladly do anything to pacify and soothe her wounded mother--anything but give up Walter; and that was the only thing which would be of any avail. She forbore to say more in his defence, however--in fact she could not have trusted her voice to keep steady or say anything just then; and as she saw the handkerchief still at her mother's eyes, her own began to overflow. She was contrite, without attempting to particularise on what account, and very unhappy.

Mrs Naylor saw that her demonstration had told, and made haste to improve the advantage. She put her handkerchief back in her pocket and cleared her voice.

"It is for your own sake I am so solicitous, Margaret. It is you he is trying to marry. You can marry but once, remember. Think how momentous is this step you are so blindly eager to take. Your whole future life depends on it."

"We are fond of one another, mother, and he is good and true. What more can a girl want?"

"Much, my dear. You talk like an inexperienced simpleton. How differently you will look on things in ten years' time! People cannot live--perhaps for fifty years--like turtles in a nest, in one continued round of billing and cooing.

They must eat and dress themselves every day; and to do that nicely takes a deal of money, more than your friend is likely ever to earn."

"I do not want to be rich. The rich people we know are not so nice, I am sure. Few of them are gentlemen."

"I know, my dear. I understand you perfectly. Love in a cottage, and that sort of thing. When I was a girl, the novels were full of it, and it was very pretty. The novels are much more sensible nowadays, and it is strange that the young people who read them should still be as foolish as ever."

"I do not think life without love would be worth the having."

"Of course not, my shepherdess! It would be charming to sit in the woods always, holding a crook tied with nice fresh blue satin ribbon, and a straw hat cocked on one side, a pet lamb at one's feet, and a swain beside one to whistle tunes upon a reed, like the Dresden-china figures; but when a shower came, and the ribbons got wet, it would be but a draggle-tailed diversion, believe me. Remember the old saying, 'When poverty comes in at the door, love flies out of the window.' You can't make love on an empty stomach. Housekeeping knocks a deal of the romance out of life."

"Walter has money, mother. With mine added, we shall be quite well off."

"I think, Margaret, if I had been pleading a gentleman's cause, I would not have put him in the invidious light of requiring a wife's fortune to enrich him. It sounds mercenary. Not that I wish to speak unkindly of your friend; but he lays himself open to the suspicion of fortune-hunting, by running after a girl with your prospects. Your uncle is not likely to marry, and you might look so very much higher, if you only had common-sense."

"I don't know where I should look for 'higher.' You have always said that his people were an excellent family in England."

"We are Canadians, my dear. Good connections in England will not help him much with us, unless they are bankers. He is a younger son, and his brother has children, so his prospect of ever coming to the family property is not worth counting. He has got all they can afford to give him, and is a fixture on this side the Atlantic for life."

"He is better off than most young men. Yet see how quickly some of them get on, and rise to the top."

"*He* will never rise, my dear. He has not been trained for getting on in this country. He will not spend as little as our young men do, and he has not the first idea of how to make a fortune."

"He would not be half as nice if he had."

"My dear, you talk like a child. When people advance into middle life, mere lovemaking grows to be up-hill work. It would be grotesque, if it had not become too insipid for people to attempt keeping it up. The larger interests are needed to make middle life bearable. It is gratifying then to find that one has married a man of note--some one heard of everywhere, and spoken of by everybody. With your looks and accomplishments and prospects, there is no man you may not have the refusal of. How comfortable, when one grows elderly and uninteresting, to be wife of the chief-justice, or of a senator, and receive as much attention in old age as one has been accustomed to in youth! An ex-beauty poorly married is a disappointed and a discontented woman, let me tell you."

"Walter could go into politics if he liked; and if he ever does, he must rise to the top, he is so clever and well informed."

"Not he. He will never be more than he is now. He is too much of an Englishman, and too fixed in his notions, ever to catch the tone of his neighbours."

"He is a gentleman. Why should he take the tone of people less cultured than himself?"

"He won't. That's where the trouble is. And therefore his neighbours will never really like him. They will fancy he looks down on them. They will never send him to Parliament, mark my words, however hard he may try. If they elect him reeve of his township, or a school-trustee, it is the most they will ever do for him.

"Playing country gentleman does not answer, my dear. It has been often tried. I have seen so many half-pay officers and others buy land, and start as country gentlemen, and it always ended the same way. In a few years their ready money was spent, and they could not move away. Their farms were worse cultivated than their neighbours', and less productive; and their children, rough and unkempt, grew up neither one thing nor another--neither gentle nor simple--with the pretensions of a class which did not care to accept them, and without the industry and thrift to keep them up in the one into which they were sinking.

"Have nothing to do with the land in this country, my dear; or marry a greedy and hard-working clown at once. Your children, at least, may come to be somebody in that case, though you will lead a drudge's life yourself."

"I am ready to risk it, mother, however it may turn out. A crust in the woods with the man of my choice, rather than all the splendour you can mention, without him."

"You are infatuated! Reason is thrown away on you. I wonder at my own patience in attempting to argue with you so long. But at least you shall not ruin your life if I can help it. If you will not send away this pernicious young man, I must carry you away from him. He shall find that however his persecution may inconvenience us, it shall further his schemes not a jot.... You will pack up to-morrow, girls, first thing. Come down to breakfast in your travelling dresses. We leave by the first train tomorrow forenoon;" and so saying, she left the room.

"Oh, Margaret!" sighed Lucy in despair; "and we had the prospect of such a good time before us."

"What could I have said, Lucy, except what I did?"

"I don't know; but it is awfully disgusting."

CHAPTER XII.

TO NAHANT?

It was about three in the morning. The lights had been extinguished in the ball-room, and the house was still. The casements of sleeping-rooms were darkening one by one as their inmates composed themselves to rest. A footfall on the gallery outside mingled with the tick of the clock on the staircase, which, in the stillness of the hour, sent monotonous vibrations through the timbers of the wooden house.

Backward and forward the walker paced, diffusing the thin smoke of his cigar upon the salt-smelling air. It was cool and even chilly as morning drew near. Already the sky had grown pale low down beyond the sea. The waters by contrast had grown more black and forbidding; and with the regular steady growl of the rollers breaking on the beach, it seemed like a monster watching at the portals of the day.

Backward and forth paced Joseph Naylor, too wakeful to sleep, and without even a wish to turn in. There was nothing painful in his ruminations, nothing to agitate; and no point of difficulty had arisen on which it was necessary for him to decide. Looking at himself in that state of divided consciousness in which one half the mind notes and surveys the workings of the other, he appeared scarcely to think at all. There was little of sequence or progress in the images among which he drifted, and the faculties of judging, choosing, desiring, intending, were not in use. There was rather a feeling of contented fruition overhanging his spirit like a golden mist, in which he seemed to bathe and be at rest.

Far back, before he had learned sorrow, he had known this sense of peace, a glimpse of Paradise from which he had been snatched away, and the gates closed after him with a clang. Looking seaward, the black expanse spread out, with low reverberating sound, seemed a symbol of his long-drawn years of desolation, a barrier between him and the faintly brightening east. To-night he seemed to overpass that gulf, and feel again the blessedness of a young bridegroom--without a wish, because he touched the goal of his desires, swimming in contentment, and breathing the scent of orange-flowers and garlands. He seemed to be inhaling it even now.

There had been a time when to recall these feelings would have driven him mad--when he had set his teeth, and turned his mind away from the memory of what had grown to be an agony, and which dogged him night and day like the remorse of some great crime. As time wore on, his life had grown more tolerable, in grey and joyless wise, with the aftermath of sober peace which sedulous virtue can rear even on the stubble of youth's luxuriant crop cut down and borne away. Yet even then, to finger the old wounds was to make them bleed anew--to remember the past was to recall his sorrow.

To-night, what change had come over him? He seemed living again in the happiness of the bygone time. He felt young as he had not felt in twenty years. He could dwell on the old joys and feel no sting; recall the image of his lost without a pang--so young and tender, with her soft brown eyes and clinging touch lingering still so kindly on his retentive sense. There was no feeling of loss to-night, no raging pang of impotent hungry jealousy.

He seemed dwelling in the fragrance of her presence; and the image of his new friend, his deliverer, was with him too, so like and yet so different from the other. The sunny warmth in those full brown eyes had beamed on him with a reviving and invigorating glow, which had thawed and quickened his poor frost-bound nature like the coming of another spring. How different the two images were! And yet, when he strove to separate and compare them in his mind, how strangely they ran together, and blended like fluid shapes into something vaguely sweet and dear, which would not be resolved into either definite form!

A hand was laid lightly on his shoulder, and he turned his head, preoccupied still with the images of his waking dream.

"I have found you at last, and at leisure," said a voice at his elbow. "You have been so busy all the evening, and I could not turn in till I had had a word with you."

"Walter! You? What is it?"

"What is this about going to Boston to-morrow? Margaret is as much taken by surprise as I am."

"Going to Boston? I know nothing of it. What do you mean?"

"Mrs Naylor told Margaret in my hearing they were going to Boston to-morrow."

"We came here intending to remain a month at least. Our rooms are only taken for a fortnight, to be sure, in case we should not like it; but if we do-- and I thought we were getting on nicely--we were to stay. At least that was my idea. But--ah! I see--Walter, you scamp! This comes of your unexpected appearance. You should be ashamed of yourself--disturbing a quiet family in this fashion. What a dangerous character you must be, when the sight of you frightens a middle-aged lady so much that she is going to pack up and run away, before--before----Bless my soul! how many days have we been here? It seems a long time, but it is not a week, not four---- We have been here only two days!

"Yes; now I think of it, my sister has been hovering round me a good deal this evening. I daresay she has been trying to get speech of me. And I was conceited enough to think it was unwarrantable curiosity on the part of Mrs Caleb, watching what I was about."

"You *were* a little different from your usual to-night, Mr Naylor. I never saw you mind young ladies much before. Tonight it has been impossible to get hold of you."

"That may have been the young ladies' fault, my boy. It is not every one of them who knows how to be good company. Naturally, a man at my time of day is less susceptible to the pink and white in a schoolgirl's face than you young fellows are. There is a time for bread and butter, and a time for other things. Solomon says so."

"I don't think any one should call Margaret a bread-and-butter miss," Walter answered, hotly.

"Margaret is a good girl, and smart--though perhaps I should not say so, who remember her a squealing baby--but she would not care to waste her evening in amusing an old uncle, when the fiddlers were around, and so many young fellows to mind her."

"And what about Boston, then? Do you mean to go? Or will you allow Mrs Naylor to take her daughters there, and break up the very pleasant party here?"

"I do not see that Mrs Caleb's going to Boston would break up the party here;" and there was a tone in Joseph's voice, as he said it, which betokened a smile, though there was not light enough to see it. "It is natural that she should want to get her girls away from a too fascinating detrimental.

"You are a sad fellow, Walter--running about the world to frighten fond mothers, and compromise the prospects of young ladies."

"I can afford to marry, Mr Naylor. You know it. You know all about my circumstances and my connections. You have admitted to me that I might fairly enough go in and win if I could."

"I am not the girl's mother, my good fellow. If I recollect aright, I said 'Wait.' That is what I would say to you again, after the lapse of hardly three months. Your patience seems to me of the shortest. You must wait, my boy--wait."

"Wait till another fellow comes forward and unsettles her mind! Stand aside, and let him step in and win her! Would you do that yourself?"

"I don't know. You speak from the gentleman's point of view, you see. It is from the lady's side, and with a view to her interests, that I must consider things. Her mother's feeling is perfectly natural. It is from no objection to yourself that she wishes to stave you off. Margaret has seen nothing of the world. It is fair that she should know what she is giving up if she marries a backwoodsman."

"She does not object to the backwoods."

"She has seen too little of life in the front to realise what she would be giving up. You have influenced her fancy, and she sees with your eyes for the moment. By-and-by she might think differently, and if it were too late it would be bad for you both. You must really have patience, and give her time."

"But----"

"Oh yes; there is plenty to say on the other side, Walter. You and I might talk a long time, but I fear neither would convince the other. Meanwhile, it is time we were both in bed. The lights are going out all over the house. Good night."

Joseph took his candle and went up-stairs. The light from a door ajar fell on him as he threaded the dim corridor, bordered with boots of sleeping guests.

"Joseph!" in a vehement whisper reached his ears. He turned, and his sister-in-law, in dressing-gown and shawl, stood before him.

"How late you are of retiring! I have watched and waited for your passing till I am completely knocked up. Ah! my poor back! and my head aches dreadfully."

"Get to bed. Late hours are always hurtful."

"I could not lie down till I had seen you. I *must* speak to you. And you have lingered so long."

"We cannot talk here--disturbing people, and being overheard. You are scarcely in trim for the parlour. Besides, the lights are out. It is very late, and I am awfully sleepy."

"Come in here. Improper?--Dear me!" and Mrs Naylor smiled sarcastically. "Our age will save our characters, Joseph, I should think. However, I will leave the door open."

"Well?" asked Joseph, following in reluctantly, "what is it--which will not keep till morning? Let's cut it as short as possible."

"Do you know that young Blount is here?"

"Yes."

"What are we to do?"

"I see no occasion to do anything."

"He may have Margaret engaged and committed any half-hour they are alone together."

"If she is willing, I do not see why he should not."

"Joseph Naylor! Is that the interest you take in poor Caleb's fatherless daughter? And you call yourself her guardian!"

"Well? What would you have me do?"

"Remove us at once. Then she is not compromised by any exhibition of intimacy there may have been this evening. I have been thinking of Nahant. It is an extravagant place, I know; but we can stop and have a couple of days' shopping in Boston on the way. Will you arrange for our starting by the forenoon train?"

"To-morrow morning! Do you forget that your rooms here are engaged for a fortnight?--could not have got them for a shorter time--and there are still eleven days to run?"

"I know. We must pay for the fortnight, of course. Another obligation to add to the many we owe your favourite."

"But you will find Nahant dull, I fear. It is not a place many Canadians go to, and you have no New England friends. Will it not be lonesome for you and the girls to look on at the gaieties, without even a man to stand beside you in the crowd?"

His sister-in-law turned and looked at him questioningly. Joseph, as she knew, was not aggressively self-asserting, but this was self-effacement beyond any modesty she could have believed.

"You will do very nicely, Joseph," she said, encouragingly. "You are presentable anywhere, and--well--almost distinguished-looking, let me tell you; and you give our party far more weight than if you were younger. And then you are so clever about making friends with the nicest people within reach. We shall do capitally."

Joseph opened his eyes and smiled, to hear his sister-in-law sum him up to his face so patronisingly. "You are too appreciative of my small merits, Susan. Pray spare me. But I had no idea of joining in your escapade. Clam Beach is perfectly good enough for me. I shall not dream of leaving it before my fortnight is up; and quite likely, if I continue to like it, I shall stay on for three or four weeks longer."

"Do you mean that you will let us roam away over the United States--your poor dead brother's helpless widow and orphans--without a protector? I could not have believed it, Joseph. But--ah! I can see it all!--designing girl--this evening----"

Mrs Naylor grew disjointed and confused, and finally stuck fast in the middle of a sentence which she could not properly be said to have begun; having merely betrayed, in her irritation, a wish "to carry the war into Africa"--or at least, since Joseph was so unsympathetic in her concerns, to discuss his own in a similar spirit. But there came the look into his face of a man who will not be trifled with, and who chooses to introduce the subject himself, when his affairs are to be mentioned; and between surprise, and having nothing exactly to say--though in another mood there would have been an opening for banter and insinuation--the thread of her ideas gave way, and she stopped short.

Joseph's brow cleared as quickly as it had darkened, so soon as Susan had checked herself; but he said nothing, and after waiting in silence for a minute and a half, he turned on his heel, saying--

"That is all you have to tell me, I suppose? Good night."

"Stop, Joseph! You have told me nothing. What am I to do? Do you really mean that you will not come with us?"

"That is what I mean."

"You propose to keep us here against our will, and to hand that poor misguided child Margaret over to such a fate? I would not have believed it of you, Joseph."

"I have no power to keep you here against your will, Susan, any more than you have the right to drag me away against mine. If I can do anything short of that to pleasure you, name it. My cheque-book is freely at your service, if you insist on going to Nahant, where you will find your expenses ten times as heavy as here."

"I don't want your cheque-book. Poor Caleb took care we should be provided for. And very fortunate it is, too,"--which was an ungracious and uncalled-for observation; but all things, as Joseph thought, are pardonable in an angry woman.

"And what am I to do," she continued, "with this young man? He will drive me distracted. I know he will."

"Accept what you cannot prevent, Susan; and save yourself the worry of struggling against the inevitable. Let them have their way. Do it soon, and make a favour of it; and you will be in a position to stipulate for long delay.

When Walter is a year or two older, he will have had enough of the wilds, and be willing to settle down in a civilised neighbourhood."

"But Margaret ought to do so much better. I cannot resign myself to the idea of her sinking into a farmer's wife. I have a right to expect position for her-- the best the Province can afford. Why should she not live in Toronto and lead society?"--which, perhaps, you may deem a small ambition, my British reader; yet it is precisely what all mankind are born to feel. Ambition is the same everywhere, but its object varies with the latitude and longitude. There are actually people as eager to be first in Timbuctoo and Bokhara, as any one you may know to be of the best in London.

"As Blount's wife," answered Joseph, "she will be all right socially; and between what she has from her father, and what she may look for from her uncle, she does not need to consider whether her husband is a rich man or not."

"I intended her to be in the middle of everything. For what else did I take so much trouble with her education?"

"She does not seem to mind about that herself."

"And there were chances for her here, if Blount would have stayed away. There is that clever Mr Wilkie, and young Walter Petty, both evidently well inclined to her."

"I think Margaret's preference shows good taste and good sense. Blount is a gentleman, and his people have a property in Wales. If you want connection, he is the best of the three."

"He is a younger son. His prospects don't amount to much, or he would have stayed at home; while Mr Wilkie----"

"A worthy person. A rising man, if you like----"

"Mrs Petty would give her eyes to get him for Ann."

"Very likely. But he is not to compare with Blount; though I do not blame him for that. There is a kind of person which must be born and bred, though it is not the kind which makes its way in the world the best. For myself, I sympathise with Margaret's taste."

"I declare, I think that young fellow has turned your head! But he *shan't* be your nephew, for all his scheming, if I can prevent it.... If you will not take us to Nahant, I suppose we must stay here. We would have to invent so many excuses if we went straight back home; though it would be serving Margaret just right if we did. But she shall stay at my side and under my eye while we remain here; Mr Blount shall gain nothing by it. The worry and botheration will injure me, I know, and may even have the worst consequences; but it will be your fault, Joseph Naylor, and some day, when it is too late, you will regret it. I would not have believed that it was in you to be so unkind."

"Good night," said Joseph, getting away at last; and before many minutes more, he too was one of the army of sleepers.

CHAPTER XIII.

MAIDA SPRINGER.

The succeeding week was a time of depression, waiting, watching, and general tantalisation for Margaret Naylor and Walter Blount. Margaret's mother was more cross and more watchful than Argus or duenna had ever been before. The only consolation--as Joseph, pitying the lad's despair, found with some remorse that he had let fall--was, that such preternatural vigilance could not last; or if it did, that Margaret would be goaded to desperation and rebel.

Interchange of glances even was denied the hapless lovers. Mrs Naylor intercepted, so to speak, an œillade in its flight across the breakfast-room on the first morning of the siege, and sternly insisted that her daughter should change places forthwith to the other side of the table, and turn her back to the enemy.

To save appearances, while acting jailer on the girl, Mrs Naylor made a martyr of herself, and moved about under a load of superabundant clothing--wrapping herself in shawls and wearing a wisp of knitting upon her head on days when her brother-in-law was wishing himself a wild Indian, that he might dress in a coat of paint. Mrs Naylor was "poorly,"--she felt premonitions of ague, a threatening of neuralgia, and, of course, severe "headache"; at least so the ladies agreed, on comparing notes, after making tender inquiries--each anxious to make sure there was nothing infectious, so as to steal away quietly before the general panic and stampede which would ensue if there were.

"Just a case of general all-overishness, my dears," said Mrs Carraway, "arising from change to this bracing air, after the sickly heats of Upper Canada. I had a touch of it myself, on coming first. There is so much salt and ozone down here."

"I should say it was a case of hypochondria," observed Mrs Chickenpip, who, being serious and robust in her views, was given to cultivate truth at the expense of charity. "I am sure we do wrong in encouraging her to make-believe, by showing so much sympathy. If you had seen, as I did, the breakfast she made this morning, you would think less of her ailments."

"That's not always a sign," said Mrs Wilkie. "Look at *me* now. I eat hearty. I'm always best at meal-times; but an hour after, I'm just fairly done, and my heart thumpin' like a smiddie hammer."

"Not at all to be wondered at," Mrs Chickenpip retorted, below her breath. "If people will over-eat, they must expect to be uncomfortable,"--a remark which passed unheard.

"How do you feel to-day, Mrs Wilkie?" was more audible. It was Rose Hillyard who spoke.

"Ah, my dear, it's you? I'm glad to see you. I'm only so-so, between the heat and the palpitations; but I think the homoeopathy is doing me good. I think the lady we are speakin' about should try some of it."

"Have you been taking any more powders?" asked Rose, smiling at the recollection of the cloud of "poother" she had seen issue from the old lady's mouth.

"Just wan each day. I haven't forgot how kind you were to me the first day. I have been better ever since."

"You blew that one all away, I think."

"It did me good all the same, my dear; and I won't forget your kindness givin' it to me. And if ever I can say a good word for you, I'll do it, ye may rely;" and the old thing actually winked, to Rose's no small indignation--on which Lettice Deane gave her a pinch in the arm, and ran away to hide her uproarious laughter.

Mrs Wilkie having dispensed her morsel of patronage, drew herself up and coughed behind her finger-tips; then, thinking that perhaps she had shown too marked a preference among candidates, she turned to Mrs Petty and inquired for Miss Ann, observing that she thought her a nice girl.

Mrs Naylor led Margaret a life which afforded her ample opportunity to repent her perverseness, had that been possible. From the time she left her room in the morning, she kept the girl at her side, to read to her when she sat, or support her with an arm when she took a walk. In the evening she kept her still at her elbow; and though she sometimes allowed her to dance, she had her back again at her side the moment the dance was ended. The other ladies were charmed and impressed by these signs of so devoted an attachment between mother and daughter, and both rose immensely in public esteem, which perhaps consoled them in their utter boredom with one another. In her heart, the mother would have liked to whip the intractable girl, while the girl, in hers, was sorely tempted to run away; but public opinion and the conventions kept both up to their pretty behaviour--and the artist's satisfaction in doing a thing really well, and being applauded for it, was assuredly an alleviation in the long and weary game of make-believe.

Mrs Wilkie praised Margaret as a good biddable girl, and confided to every one who cared to listen, "that she would be quite pleased if Peter would take a fancy to her; though, to be sure, there was that Miss Hillyard, a most superior person,--and it was doubtful to which he would incline." Mrs Petty thought her the sweetest-tempered heiress she had ever seen, wished she could secure her for her boy Walter, and became the inseparable companion of mother and daughter.

By the third day of Mrs Naylor's sickness, she found herself the recipient of so much attention, that she became quite reconciled to her *rôle*--liked it almost--and might, I suppose, be taken as of that curious class of people of whom it is recorded in newspapers that they "enjoy poor health." Mrs Petty fairly laid siege to the regard of mother and daughter, and old Mrs Wilkie sought the society of the two mothers, who paid her unlimited attention in return, each protesting to the other that it was quite a lark to quiz the simple soul, while both were devoutly hoping that she would accept their blandishments in good faith, and influence her son accordingly. Soon other ladies joined the coterie--Mrs Deane with Lettice and Rose, and others; and then bachelors began to hover on the confines of the circle--till the sick lady's chair became a centre for whatever was going on.

Walter Blount growled at being of those outside, and was very down-hearted, though he struggled his best. He cultivated his favoured rival Walter Petty, waylaid Lucy, who was not under surveillance, several times a-day, and intrusted her with messages to her sister. There was Joseph, too, from whom he could extract sympathy at least; and then there was the sight of his charmer's back hair, always in view at the dinner-table, reminding him how near she was, "if still so far"--which was something, but not enough; and after a week, he removed his base of operations to Lippenstock, a few miles along the coast, where, being out of sight, he could mitigate the severity of Margaret's durance, though still within touch of whatever went on at Clam Beach.

He might have had others, who would have been happy to distract his thoughts, but he could think only of the one, and was indifferent to other society; whence it arose that he spent a good deal of his time alone, and interested many a tender heart in his behalf.

"Who can he be?" Fanny Payson asked Lettice Deane. "And what is the matter with him? Did you ever see so young a fellow, so handsome and so down in the mouth, at a watering-place before? *I* never did. He should turn hermit, or join the Shakers. They live quite near. He is no sort of use here, and quite out of place. He minds nobody, and I am sure I have given him every chance."

"He is not altogether a stranger. He has friends here. He knows the Naylors. I see him sometimes with Lucy, and he is often with the uncle, whom Rose Hillyard has chosen to inthral. I suspect he is only a retiring young man, and painfully shy. What would you say to our taking him in hand, and teaching him how nice he might become? He is a fine manly-looking fellow, and our hands are not very full just now. It would make us feel 'kind o' useful in our generation,' as my uncle Zebedee says, to draw him out. Suppose you and I form ourselves into a Geneva Red Cross Branch Society, to cure his bashfulness, and teach him how to flirt."

"It can't be done, Lettice. I have tried, and I guess you'll allow I'm a qualified practitioner. The trouble I've taken! And all for nothing. I should feel downright mean about it, if I wasn't sure the man's a loon."

"What brings him to Clam Beach, I wonder?"

"That I can't imagine. But he's of no account here. He evidently believes his eyes were only given him to see with; as for *looking*, he has no more notion of it than a stone wall. I have given him the very nicest and most varied opportunities--you know he sits opposite me at table. I have tried every variety of assault, from pensive up to arch, and he seems absolutely impervious. I doubt even if he could distinguish me from the chair I sit on, and yet I have gone so far as actually to ask him to pass the butter. He just looks steadily past me, as if his attention was fixed on what went on at the table behind."

Maida Springer likewise observed the young misanthrope, felt interested in him, and discussed him with Mrs Denwiddie. "He has a history, that young man," she would say; and she would sigh as she said it, as if to imply that there were others who had histories as well. "It's a heart history too, and not a happy one; and he has just come here, I do believe, to try if he can't learn to bear it. He is seeking to drown memory with sounds of mirth and fashionable dissipation; but he finds it a hollow mockery, just as others have done, and he wanders down upon the wave-beat shore, and listens to the ever-sounding sea, and it kind o' calms him, and he comes back feelin' better--just like the rest. Ah yes!--as I have done myself."

"You, my dear, with a history? Ah yes! to be sure. You mentioned it one day. Your friend went away without proposin', I think you said? It may have been mean of him--I can't say; or it may have been a mistake of your own. Girls are so ready to fool themselves that way. It don't folly that the man was in fault. If a man only passes them the apple-sarse with a smile, there are women who will call it a particular attention."

"I didn't mention anything of the kind," the other answered tartly, turning to go away; but no one of her friends whom she could join was in sight, so she changed her intention, and proceeded to bestow on her cross-grained companion "a bit of her mind."

"You appear to think it a grand thing to have been able to get yourself married, Mrs Denwiddie, and you seem disposed to look down on every young woman who is still single; but you don't tell what *kind* of man you got, and you forget that if everybody was willing to take what offered, there would be no single folks left. We may have been too particular, we single women, but the married ones have no call to despise us for that."

"No offence, my dear," said Mrs Denwiddie, who really could not afford to quarrel with her chief intimate. "I was just speaking in the gineral."

"And so was I, ma'am; and don't you forget it. I'm going home on Friday, and as there's few you are likely to pick up with much when I'm gone, except the single ladies, I would strongly recommend you to respect their feelin's, and not brag too much about havin' been married. They could have been married too, if they'd have took what offered--like some others."

"Hoity-toity, my dear! I said 'no offence.' But you're all that tetchy, you old--hm--but never mind. I'm sorry you're going. I for one will miss you. I did not think the schools at Montpelier took up so soon. I expected that you and me would have been leaving at the same time, in about three weeks."

"I have arrangements to make at our ladies' college. They are adding a class of Metaphysics and Political Economy, and Miss Rolph, our principal, says I would get it if I wasn't so young."

"And well you would teach economy too, my dear, to judge by the neat way your gloves and slippers is mended. And it's a thing girls have much need to learn, if only there was some one who knew it; but the mothers of town-bred girls are ez extravagant mostly ez themselves. But how old must a woman be before she is qualified to teach economy? Strikes me, if they don't know it when they're young, they'll never know it."

"This is metaphysics and political economy. That means running the State, not household management. Miss Rolph's establishment is devoted to the higher culture. We leave the affairs of common life to elementary schools. Miss Rolph says a woman should be forty and a formed character before she ventures to instil these grand subjects into the American woman of the future. I won't be thirty till my next birthday."

"You don't mean that, my dear? You'll be a married woman, I hope, before you're old enough to go lecterin' about physic, on them terms. And I don't hold with women-doctors, let me tell you. They hain't got strength in their arms to pull out a good-sized tooth; and as for intelleck, I can't abide a woman of intelleck. But you're different, my dear, and you're young yet--in a way; and you do yourself injistice, let me tell you. What makes you dress so severe? A veil would save your eyes as good as them blue glasses you wear out of doors, and be a sight more becomin'. You can't expect to fetch a young man with a look that comes filterin' to him through coloured glass. And I'd put on more style, if I was as young as you, my dear, and buy me a new *jupong* out of Bosting. There's nothing like stylish clothes, my dear, when you're young; and you'll never be younger."

Maida felt positively grateful and soothed at the old woman's prattle. It takes so very small a crumb of personal interest to cheer and warm the hearts of lonely ones. The schoolma'am was by herself in the world, earning her own living, and battling her solitary way in life. Those among whom she lived employed her at what she could do, paid her, and that was the end of it. They had their own concerns and interests. When Maida's work was done, they let her go her way,--a drop in the river, a unit in the crowd, into whose life they were not called on to intrude, and who would have shrunk from pushing herself into theirs. She could have kissed Mrs Denwiddie, had the situation been more favourable; as it was, she drew closer to her in their walk upon the sands, rubbing against her dumbly, as the animals do when they find a friend, and felt warmed in doing it.

Mrs Denwiddie understood, and a motherly instinct awoke within her, which was new and pleasant--a fresh interest in the monotony of a life in which the bells for meals had been the only landmark.

CHAPTER XIV.

SUNSET AND MOONSHINE.

Friday arrived, the omnibus came round to the door, and Maida Springer bade Mrs Denwiddie farewell. Circumstances had made these two intimate, though they had little in common. Both were solitary, and neither had the talent of attracting strangers. They were a mutual resource, keeping each other in countenance, and enabling both to mix in the general company without the apologetic feeling which either would have experienced had she been alone. They had grown to have a kindness for each other; and it was with quite a warm embrace and a moistening of the eye that they parted, each feeling the world emptier for the absence of the other.

The omnibus started in the afternoon, trundling leisurely along the quiet country roads, stopping here and there by the way to put down or take up baskets and an occasional passenger; and on reaching Narwhal Junction it remained there for some hours, till a train from the North, another from the South, and a third going West, should all have come in.

Maida procured a paper at the bookstall, and sat down on the platform to await her train, which was the latest of the three. There was not much in the paper--there never is, when one tries to read it against time; but there were a few arrivals and departures by the other trains, to break the tedium; and as the dusty afternoon wore by, and the lengthening purple shadows stole out from their lurking-places in the woods and under the hill-tops, there was enough to interest any one who had eyes to see.

The Junction stood on a middle level, near the edge of a wide extent of cultivated land which sloped down towards a quiet river flowing away behind; and beyond that were low swelling hills, covered with woods, shining like bronze where they caught the slanting light, and melting into waves of blue below the horizon. In front, toward the south-west, the land sloped up to meet the shadows of overhanging thickets, dipping down on the right where a brook in its rocky dell escaped from the mountain country farther back, filling the air with sound, and babbled onward to the river among the fields. Hills shaggy with bush and boulder concealed the streamlet's source; and behind, a heaven-piercing peak lifted its reddened profile to the light, while blue dim greyness veiled its storm-scarred bosom. A mile distant, on the right, the village of Narwhal, with its little tin steeple twinkling like a star, was seated where the brook and river met, weltering with its surrounding fields in a haze of gold and crimson, with purpled woods behind, and all the glorious pomp of sinking day above it and beyond--the saffron-coloured sky, the waiting flakes of cloud, flashing in scarlet fire to let the sun-god pass, and then to draw the curtain on his exit.

The level crimson rays shot for a space along the glorified valley, kindling the distant reaches of the river into flame, and impurpling the long-drawn shadows with the hue of violets; and then the pageant vanished like a dream. Cool, low-toned greys stole out along the river; the rosy day-dream of the village paled into common wreaths of thin blue smoke; the starry twinkle of the steeple-vane went out in a moment, like an extinguished spark. The cirrhus clouds high up in the zenith, or far off in the cool east, still showed a rosy tint; but excepting these, the war of the giants--the ever-recurring tragedy of light and darkness--had played itself to an end. Already the shadows of the night were out among the hills, and stealing down in troops to overspread the land.

Maida stood and watched the spectacle. She was abundantly read in the literature of the magazines. The Solar Myth had always impressed her, and now the pomp of sunset recalled the story of Herakles, enthralled in Nessus' shirt, leaping on the altar and vanishing in flame. "The end of a hero!" she whispered to herself, there being no one else to hear--though, if there had been, it would have made no difference. Being a free-born American, she felt no false shame about giving utterance to her thoughts, however high-stepping they might sound at times. If her auditor did not appreciate, it only showed his dulness.

She had removed her spectacles some time before, when the daylight grew less glaring. Her hat was pushed back, and her hair rumpled out of its usual primness. The pinched, worn, and disappointed set of her features--the livery of hard-worked governesses--was lost for the moment in the sweet light reflected from the rosy clouds, and the natural intelligence always dwelling in her eyes was now warmed into enthusiasm over the drama of the elements. She looked pleasing, and even pretty, for the moment--her figure slight and girlish, rather than skinny, as it had appeared at times under the trying contrasts of the crowded hotel. In the elation of her feelings she stood erect with head well up, and altogether different from the neglected schoolma'am of other times. Wherever the divine gift of intelligence resides, there are possibilities of beauty; and the mantle of the flesh at times will fall into graceful lines, even though the buffetings of circumstance may toss and twist it awry in the general. We are lamps of clay through which the inner brightness shines more or less clearly; and it is or the flame's being trimmed, or burning low, that good looks worth the having mostly depend.

There was a whistle up the track, and presently, with a tempestuous rush which made the station tremble, a train swept up to the platform and stopped. A big bell was jangled in front of the dining-room, and nasal voices yelled--"Narwhal Junction! Twenty minutes for ree-freshment!" The passengers alighted and hurried across the platform, and Maida bade adieu to her musings and hastened to get her luggage checked for her journey.

A gentleman was coming from the distant end of the train. He too was hastening, but in the opposite direction. Both were intent on their own affairs, the platform was crowded, and ere they knew it, each was in the other's arms. Both recoiled, and stood to recover breath and apologise. Both looked. Both started in surprise.

"Gilbert Roe!" It was the lady who was the first to speak.

"Maida----?" responded the gentleman, and then he looked apologetic. He might be taking a liberty, he thought, and looked about to see if there was a husband to resent so familiar a use of his wife's name. "Are you travelling alone?" he asked, after a minute's silence, during which the lady's eyes had been so intently busy with him that she forgot to speak.

"You look older," she said at last. "Of course you must, after ten years' absence; but you are only improved--broad-chested and prosperous-looking;" and she wrung his hand in an intensity of welcome. "Where are you travelling to? What a strange place to meet in! Were you coming to----" but she did not finish her sentence. It occurred to her that it was her friend's turn to say something now.

"I am on my way to Clam Beach," he answered. "I shall put in a few days there, and then try some of the other places along the coast. Have been at several already. Not much account, any of them; but this is the season for being away. Nothing astir in Chicago at this time of year."

"Clam Beach? I've come from there. You'll find it pleasant. The house is full; but of course they can put up a single gentleman."

"You are there? Come, that's nice! I declare I'm in luck at last. My trip has been real lonesome, so far. I have been so long West that I have lost sight of my old friends, and can't scare up one, now I want 'em."

"You don't deserve to, if you serve them all as you did me. How many years is it since you wrote last, do you think? It's eight."

"Eight years? Ah, well, but that is different," he answered, with a laugh. "Who is with you at Clam Beach?"

"Who would be? The teachers at our college are mostly home with their friends. I'm an orphan, as you know, and I don't make very free with strangers; so I come to the shore, like other folks who have no friends to visit;" and she heaved a little sigh, but not a painful one. If life had been rather empty for her, that was forgotten now; "over," I daresay she would have said just then, if her feelings had fallen into words, for her eyes were on his face, her lips were parted, and her countenance was alight, more brightly than when the sunset clouds had lit it up a while ago. This was a rosier, warmer light, shining from within. It transfigured her for the moment, casting back the gathering years with their encrusting vapours, and disclosed her again as the enthusiastic maiden from whom the young man had parted ten years before, but purified and brightened by the struggles, and the victories, and the wisdom painfully acquired--for the moment, that is: there are no tabernacles or abiding-places on our mounts of transfiguration, and their glories are evanescent.

"You mean that you are still unmarried? Strange!"

"Strange that a woman should keep her troth, Gilbert? There came no word of your death. I only had patience--only waited, just as any right woman would have done."

"Hm----" It was not the answer which Gilbert had anticipated, if indeed he anticipated any. It startled him, and made him look more carefully in her face. Illuminated by the momentary exaltation of her nerves, she really looked attractive then, and there was a glowing warmth in her eyes resting on his own which thrilled him, and held him in a spell not to be shaken off, though he tried. It turned back the pages of his memory and opened a far-back chapter where ardent passages were inscribed--a chapter broken off in the middle; and then a leaf had been turned, and new chapters with new interests and new ardours had written themselves in--the stirring interests and eager ardours of an intenser life--and the old chapter had remained unfinished, and even the part written had been forgot.

Now, the old passage was again before him, and he felt a drawing back to the old-time idyl, and an impulse to carry it on and complete it. Yet there was a thinness in this proffered draught of love, which did not now as of old attract his sophisticated palate. It seemed like whey to the shepherd's son who has sojourned in cities and revelled in stronger drinks--wholesome, but not exhilarating. The bowl was at his lips, but he hesitated to drink. His glance waxed unsteady beneath the gaze of blissful trust which beamed on him. He coughed again to break the confusing silence, and would have spoken, but he could think of nothing to say.

And then the damsel's look grew clouded, in sympathy with, or in consequence of, his confusion; and with a little gasping sob and a tighter clutch at his hand, which she still was holding, she spoke, half whispering--

"And you? You--you are not married, Gilbert?" and her eyes rose shrinkingly to his face, with an eager frightened look, as if she dreaded to hear his answer.

"N--no--that is--no--certainly not! What makes you suppose such things? I have no thought----Tush! you put me out asking ridiculous questions. I forget what I am saying;" and he laughed uneasily, looking most unnecessarily confused over so simple an avowal.

His confusion was unnoticed, however. Maida looked up in his face once more, as trustingly as ever; or more so, for now there was the triumph of proud possession. Her ten years' waiting was accomplished; her love was come to claim her. The stony road she had been travelling so wearily and alone, was behind her now. It grew radiant in retrospect by the light of the joy she had now attained, even as the toils of battle seem glorious in the lustre of the victory which they have achieved. Her love was come to claim her! She stood up closer and looked into his face, with upturned lips, awaiting the seal of their reunion.

It did not come. The omnibus was drawing up at the platform, and Gilbert, calling a porter, turned away to point out his luggage. Maida went in pursuit of her own, and to the surprise of the driver, had it restored to the place on the roof whence it had been lifted an hour or two before, and then followed Gilbert inside, to return to Clam Beach.

CHAPTER XV.

IN AN OMNIBUS.

The daylight was stealing swiftly yet imperceptibly away. There was no moon, and the occupants of the omnibus were speedily wrapped in gloom. Besides the two we know of, there were others sitting in silence, and in wait for anything to amuse them on the monotonous journey. The vehicle rolled easily along the sandy road, without noise or jar to drown the sound of conversation, and Maida dared not give voice to the many things with which her happy heart was overflowing, before the inquisitive strangers, while Gilbert was far from indisposed to hold his tongue.

To participate with enthusiasm in a *réchauffé* of feeling, after ten years, and in other scenes and circumstances, demands an effort. If the feeling has been one merely of friendship, such participation is no doubt possible--nay, the long interval lends an atmosphere of pensive charm to the revival, clothes it in roseate hues, and tempts one, in looking down the vista of the years, to see the bond as closer than it really was. But if the friendship was one "touched with emotion," as it mostly is when the parties are a young man and a maid, it is different. The aroma of such a tie is far too subtle and evanescent to survive much keeping. Cherish the memories ever so carefully, as Maida had done, it is only like the storing away of roseleaves. The perfume waxes even stronger, but it is not the same; it is musty and heavy, like spice or drugs--a mummy of the old sweet breath of flowers. Cherish not, as was Gilbert's case, and what is left? The roses have withered, the petals crumbled and blown away, and what remains but the memory of a remembrance?

Had this meeting come ten years later, when the effervescence of the emotions, and the expectation of new sweetness still to be extracted from the dregs of youth, had subsided, then doubtless it would have been pleasant to recur to a tender friendship, and to trick it out in such shreds of sentiment as could be picked from out the lumber of the past. Self-love and self-pity would have delighted to dwell on such a memento of departed youth, when the time for new attachments had passed away. But at thirty a man is still young, except to his juniors. There may yet be loves and friendships to come, more precious than any which have gone before. He looks back upon his past as a mere introduction to his full-fledged present--the raw and callow time of his probation--and early kindnesses seem pale, watery, and insipid.

Gilbert was pleased enough to meet an old friend; especially just then, when he was bound for a pleasure resort, where, as always, those who have friends are tempted to season their social enjoyments with as much exclusiveness as they can afford, and enhance the satisfaction of being within the ring, by keeping as many as possible outside. But this new-found friend claimed so much for their intimacy in the past--so much which was special and particular, and for which he really doubted in himself if there had been warrant. It was an affair of ten years ago. Since then he had led a busy life, overflowing with all the excitements; and he wondered now if there could have been ground for the meaning she appeared to attribute to it. There might have been once, or there nearly might have been--and if the intimacy had lasted longer, perhaps there *would* have been; but they had now been ten years apart, and who could resurrect a sentiment buried under ten years of oblivion? There had been time for many another tenderness since then. And were not attachments like the herbage of the fields, of which each season produces its own luxuriant crop? Besides, since then a plant more vigorous than any had sprung up, one with deeper-reaching root and wider branches, which had usurped the space and choked all weaker growths. It was a plant whose fruit had been tart as well as sweet; but the complex flavour of it had made his palate critical, and anything more luscious would be mawkish now. Again, had she not been a little abrupt? Was it nice in her to speak so openly--to step so unhesitatingly across the chasm of a ten years' separation, into a past as to which he really had forgotten the particulars? He doubted if that past had been as she would represent it; and even if it had, was it maidenly in her to be the first to speak of it?

Still, he was going amongst strangers. This old friend would be a resource, and would help to break the ice for him; and no doubt, with judgment, he would be able to lead her into seeing things as they were, instead of as she wished them to be. And after all, it was a kindly trait in her to have remembered him so long, poor girl! He hoped it had not interfered with her prospects, much, or made her measure others who were candidates for her favour by too high a standard. Yet it was well, perhaps, to have a high standard, "a noble ideal." That was the way it was expressed by the winter-evening lecturers, and the magazine writers; who, as far as he recollected, always spoke of it as "precious." And he spread himself a little wider in his dark corner of the omnibus, expanded his chest, and felt pleased with himself in the new character of "element in a woman's higher culture." Ah! what a fellow he was, to be sure! If the girls did see his perfections, poor things, it was not his fault. It showed only that they had eyes to see, and he could not wish them blind. It was impossible, of course, that he could be in love with them all; but it was consoling to think that, in being a "noble ideal," he was conferring a moral benefit on those whose attachment he could not return. And through his mind there ran the familiar lines--

"'Tis better to have loved and lost,
Than never to have loved at all."

And he sighed contentedly, feeling very kindly towards poor Maida Springer.

Maida sat in the opposite corner of the omnibus, tumultuously happy. She felt garrulous at first in her elation, but the presence of fellow-passengers--staid country folks, who did not speak, but looked inquisitively at her and her friend, as strangers in those parts, and then communicated with each other in interjectional observations about the crops--compelled her to silence; and she had so much to fill her thoughts, that soon she fell into a delightful reverie, and had no wish to converse.

As the daylight grew more dim, she lost sight of her recovered Gilbert; but there he sat before her, all the same--his outline clear against the quiet sky seen through the open window, broad-shouldered, tall and strong, a very rock of manhood; and every thread and tendril of her heart seemed to go out and twine itself around him, as she sat nestled in spirit within his shadow, in a passion of trusting adoration.

How fine of him to have kept true through all the years!--through vicissitudes and seductions such as she could not imagine or particularise, but which yet must have been most trying. And now they were re-united. And yet, how diffident and even shy he had seemed, at meeting her! and with so little to say. Depth of feeling!--to which language was too poor to give expression. It was beautiful. And what a joy for her, by-and-by, to lend his dumb soul language!--and to encourage his faltering emotions to body themselves in words.

"Douglas! Douglas! tender and true!" were the words which kept hymning themselves through her brain in a continuous rapture. Ah, what a hero! and how goodly was his shadow! It seemed but yesterday that they had parted. Ten years of dreariness, the worries and petty scufflings, small aims and smaller disappointments, which had seemed so long and dull and wearing in their passage, were all forgot and put away, like the flatness of a rainy afternoon, when it is over. She was in her teens again, strolling in the fields with Gilbert on Sunday afternoons, or reading with him on winter nights in the parlour of his uncle's homestead, when the children, her charges, were gone to bed.

The air from the fields blew in through the open windows, as the omnibus lumbered on, dewy and cool, and sweet with the scent of second-growth clover; and she thought of the humming of bees, and the sunshine and the peace of the long vacation, when Gilbert was home from college, and their talks about the world, and books, and college lore, which had been so inspiring, and had filled her with ambitions, and tempted her to break from rustic life, and work and struggle, till now she was a professor in the Female College of Montpelier. What poor dry husks it had all appeared to her but that very morning! And now it was past, clean vanished out of her life; and she felt like a moth when it casts the chrysalis and spreads its wings to sport upon the scented air. The wonder of it all! and the beauty! Now that they were past, she would not have had the times of dark probation shortened by a day.

The omnibus jogged tranquilly on its way in the sweet summer night, diverging here and there to drop a passenger at his own gate, and then resuming its course, no one remonstrating at delay or seeking to quicken the pace. The casuals were all and severally deposited at last. A little longer, and the journey was completed; the dark bulk of the hotel, with its countless lights in ranges long-drawn-out and twinkling tier on tier, a garish illumination intruding on the stillness and mystery of night, loomed up before them, and the travellers drew rein before the entrance at Clam Beach.

It was almost with regret that the two found themselves at their journey's end, so pleasant had it been; and yet they had not exchanged a word. Their musings, different as they were, had been alike pleasurably engrossing, and alike productive in each of kindness for the other. No two people could have been mutually better disposed than were Gilbert and Maida as he handed her out, and waving the porter aside, insisted on carrying in her rugs with his own hands.

"Maidy Springer! you back!" was ejaculated, as Maida reached the hall-way landing; and out of the darkness of the outside gallery swooped Mrs Denwiddie in a whirlwind of flapping drapery, enveloping Maida in a cloud of kisses and black grenadine.

"So glad to have you back again, my dear. It's been real lonesome this afternoon without you. But what has brought you? I thought you were gone to be made a doctoress of philosophy,--and here you are again; and not alone either! Is that the philosophy we study? No better than the rest, for all your learning. It's woman's subjick you incline to after all--a young man--when you can get him. Sly-boots! And me never to suspect it. It's not an hour since I was argying with that stuck-up old Mrs Wilkie, and insistin' that you was all intelleck; and here you are, back with a gentleman to disprove my words."

Maida felt doubtful how she should reply, and but for the joy which filled her she would have resented the other's inquisitive freedom. It seemed to her at that moment, however, that nothing could ever vex her more, and a reproachful look was all she could call up, by way of self-assertion.

"Well, yes, my dear," the widow answered to the look, "I'll own to it. I *am* making free. But it comes of the interest I feel in you; though many's the spat you and me has had together. But who's the gentleman? A mighty fine man. Is it HIM? the one you kind of let on about, that was away making a fortune to marry you on? Sakes alive, now! Ain't that pretty! If this ain't true love, there's no sich thing. And so little as you said! And so despondent-like you used to seem! I reely thought the whole a flam, and you just makin' believe a bit, because the gentlemen here didn't much mind you. And now, perhaps, you'll be married the first, for all the airs some tries to put on." And again she pumped Maida's hands up and down by way of congratulation.

"And now, my dear," the widow resumed, "you must make me acquainted with the gentleman himself. I'm fairly dyin' to know him. So true and so constant! I wonder if there's more like him where he comes from. I never saw the man myself would be so faithful. But maybe it's yourself, Maidy Springer, has some knack of bindin' them to you; though that's a notion never struck me before."

Maida smiled and held up her chin, while her eyes modestly sought the ground. She mentioned that she and her friend were going to supper, and if Mrs Denwiddie cared to accompany her to the dining-room, she would introduce Mr Roe. That gentleman reappearing at the moment, the three went in together, and Mrs Denwiddie's sentimental tendencies had a treat in watching over the reunion and refreshment of two faithful lovers. Her eyes dwelt on the face of the gentleman with smiles of motherly solicitude, and she ministered to his wants whenever the waiter turned his back, passing him the sugar-basin, handing him jam and pickles, and pointing out the nicest kinds of cake, in a way as troublesome as it was well intended.

Maida was in glory--too happy to eat or drink. Her credit among women was vindicated at last. Evidence of her prowess was there present; the victim, a man of six feet stature, acknowledging her silken fetters. No one would ever say "old maid" to her again, or think it. She was transferred from the forlorn to the triumphant division of her sex, and it was altogether "just too delightful." Her merit, even in her own eyes, took new proportions. How true she must have been, and constant! And she began to perceive what a very superior nature was hers, to have cherished this beloved image for ten long years. And yet, in her modesty, she had been as little aware of the tenacity of her affection as of the enduring influence of her conquering charms. To think that she could have loved and waited so long! As if, poor soul, there had since appeared in her life any man on whom to bestow the treasure of her love. She had not hoped, far less expected, this felicity. The memory of ten years back had been but the remembered gleam of sunshine in a clouded existence, to be recurred to when other women flaunted their successes before her eyes--a testimony that she, too, had had her sip of love.

Her soul overflowed with gratitude to this champion who had vindicated her equality with other women to herself and them, with humble trustful devotion.

The sensations were all so new as yet. By-and-by, doubtless, when ideas had had time to ferment, it would be different. Victorious beauty would as usual demand its dues, trifle with the captive's chains, and play at being imperious and exacting. For the present the game was all too new; she was too happy for common food, and pastured her eyes on the goodly proportions of her hero--his noble brow, his moustache, his nose, and all his manifold perfections. Timidly she pushed the buttered toast within his reach, and the anchovy paste, and watched the carefully divided mouthfuls of his meal as they were made away with.

Maida's heart was too full for speech, Gilbert's jaws were employed in mastication; wherefore they sat in silence, and Mrs Denwiddie, facing them with attentive eyes, was forced to feed her curiosity with sympathetic fancies.

"How much the poor dears must be thinking, when they speak so little! and how devoted Maida is, to be sure, pressing toast and anchovy upon her companion, and never touching a morsel herself! And what a very fine man the gentleman is, to be sure! And as for Maida herself, she really is not at all amiss--quite spry, in fact, and with a good colour, if she do be a little thin. But that will mend soon. There's nothing like a good heart to put flesh on the bones."

CHAPTER XVI.

LIPPENSTOCK BAY.

The next morning early, ere yet the last night's arrivals were astir, there was bustle in the hotel. Omnibuses, carriages, buggies, and a few saddle-horses, waited before the door, and soon a loquacious company of pleasure-seekers, comprising three-fourths of all the guests, came down and were borne away.

Joseph Naylor had the buggy which led, Rose Hillyard by his side, as nearly always happened now--though he had many competitors who strove hard to supplant him. His luck or good management was remarkable; for somehow, though the lady was conspicuously gracious and encouraging to the rest, it was nearly always to him that it fell to escort her. Lucy Naylor and Lettice Deane were provided each with a horse and a cavalier; Margaret, in her riding-habit, was following; Peter Wilkie sprang forward to hold her stirrup, but it felt so warm that she changed her mind and followed her mother into a carriage, which changeableness the latter was far from approving; but Mrs Petty was beside her, and young Walter on the box, so nothing could be said, and if Peter's mother muttered "whimsical monkey," and looked cross, nobody minded. In ten minutes every one had mounted or scrambled into a place, and the company started away.

The air was still. The sea stretched like a mirror beneath the limpid sky, repeating in livelier tones its cerulean blueness and the pearly brightness of the clouds, save near the shore, where the reflections grew troubled in the swinging of the glassy swell which broke and crumbled in a fringe of glittering surf. There was no breeze, but the sun was low as yet, and the coolness of night still lingered in the air with a pleasant saltness and the scent of fresh sea-wrack cast up along the shore. It was a charming drive, that summer morning, along the even firmness of the beach, so smooth, and free from noise, jolt, or rattle. The fall of the horses' feet was scarcely audible, and the air was astir with the plashing of the breakers in faint monotonous resonance, a low and unobtrusive accompaniment to the blithesome voices of the merry-makers as they wended along.

The motion was smooth, but the progress was not rapid. The sand was heavy beneath the wheels and the horses' feet, and offered a dead impediment to speed. But speed was not a thing to be greatly desired. The morning, with its brightness, its freshness, and its waxing warmth, was something to be lingered in, and breathed with long deep inspirations of enjoyment; and no one thought of haste or complained of delay, though it took an hour to do the five miles' distance which brought them to Lippenstock Bay and the wooden jetty, where a steamboat was waiting to take them on board. Out upon the water was a new and fresh sensation, and one which arrived just as the other was losing its charm. The sands, when they left them, were not as cool as they had been an hour before--the genial warmth was beginning to verge on heat; and the party crowded on board with enthusiasm, in haste to secure commodious corners and lounge at ease, inhaling new freshness as the boat put off from the shore with a screech like the cry of a sea-gull, and breasted the glassy waters on its voyage round the bay.

Lippenstock Bay is an inlet of eight miles' width, running deep into the land, and guarded at its mouth by a double row of islands, which shelter it from the outer ocean, breaking the lines of westward-driven billows, and rendering it a sheltered roadstead in all weathers. It cuts into the gently swelling country which comes down upon the sea, with its sandy pasture-tracks, and scattered farmhouses nestling in sheltered spots among meadows and shady trees, so snug and thrifty, but, alas for the landscape! so aglare with whitewash. If ever the spirit of the picturesque shall invade those shores, her first exploit, I fear, will be to scatter something of neglect, if not decay, upon the scene. In that transparent atmosphere, with its sharp uncompromising lights and shadows, the human element of the present is aggressively manifest. Each dwelling, in its flagrant paint or whiteness, obtrudes itself upon the eye, and insists on being counted in, one more residence of a citizen of the Great Republic. The fields and roads, the fences and blocks of bush, are scrupulously rectangular, without one softening curve: illustrated in the varying greens and yellows of the different crops, the country looks as if it were covered with a vast patch bed-quilt.

The hills of the rougher country, backed by the blue outline of distant mountains, come into view at the upper end of the bay, basking sweetly in the light, and clothed in pearly greys where their verdure falls in shadow. They relieve the scene from the sense of vulgar commonplace which the rawness of nearer objects might impose, and above is the immeasurable vault filled with transparent air suffused with brightness, including all, and reducing stretches of monotonous country within symmetrical limits. The hills behind send down a spur across the lower levels to the sea. This ends in a ridge which enters the head of the bay, and on it stands the pretty old town of Lippenstock.

Lippenstock is one of the oldest settlements on the Atlantic coast; and being old, it is rich in the mellowness of tone so sadly wanting in other places. Having grown with the community, it harmonises like a natural production with surrounding nature, free from the harsh obtrusiveness of a brand-new construction, and might almost be a cutting from the Old World ingrafted on the still scarce-ripened New. Clustered on its tongue of land, it stretches out into the blue deep water, a lesser bay margined with yellow sand confining and compacting it on either hand; fringed on three sides with wharfs, whose tar-black timbers lend a solid definition to the base from which it rises, in blocks of russet brown, red brick, and grimy stone, with roofs and steeples rising tier on tier in jagged outline backward and upward, spreading as they recede, in every tone of blue and purple grey, among the tops of the embowering elms which line the quiet streets. A ship or two is moored along the quays; for the drowsy place has considerable trade, and fishing-boats, with half-reefed umber sails and their red-shirted crews, are sleeping on the water.

The throbbing of the steamer's engine sounded far and wide across the tranquil calm, the gurgling waters parting at its bow and speeding backward in a trail of troubled undulations. The air seemed quickened into life by the motion, and fanned the voyagers gently as they reclined upon the deck, steeping themselves in sunshine, which, now they were on the water, seemed less ardent than it had been ashore.

Mrs Naylor, being an invalid, had had her choice of places. Reclining near the bow, where the air was untainted by engine-room vapours, she sat in the shadow of her white umbrella in perfect comfort, Margaret beside her, with her book and fan and other paraphernalia at hand when wanted.

At Margaret's elbow, leaning against the bulwarks, stood Walter Petty in watchful patience, waiting for something to say when opportunity should arise, though his mind felt too blank to originate an observation, while he watched and admired in a worshipful silence which ought to have gratified her if she had understood it; but she did not. She liked him as a young fellow always kind and nice, but he bored her, rather, with his superfluity of still life and lack of initiative; or, to put it plainly, she found him much too diffident and young.

He was three years older than herself, it is true, and was looked on as a wonder of readiness and knowledge by his compeers among the budding lawyers of Toronto; but then he was in love, poor lad, in his first and earliest passion, which is like the measles, and deals more hardly with a man, when, having passed him by before, it falls on him out of season. He had studied hard, and his ambition had been so entirely in his profession that he had had no thought to waste upon young ladies; and often had he scoffed and pitied, to see the ridiculous figure his fellows cut in the ecstasies of their calf-love. He had listened to their idiotic raptures of hope and despair, and wondered how rational creatures could become such fools. Now, the fate had fallen on himself. It is decreed that man shall once in his life make an ass of himself in dealing with the other sex, however wise and prudent he may be in commerce with his own; and the man who never does so stumble must be a wiseacre, or worse, an imperfect organism, from whose construction the heart or the ideal impulses have been omitted.

Walter's hot fits and cold were like an ague, and left him as limp and powerless as an ague would. The briskest and most talkative of his set at other times, he found his mind under this new influence dried up and sterile, without an idea fit to put in words, now when he was most anxious to be amusing and to shine. His being seemed turned into a pool of receptivity, absorbing the worshipped image, but unable to give back a reflection. He was happy where he stood, within range of so much sweet influence, but he was scarcely agreeable; he had nothing to say, and he still retained sufficient common-sense to feel a little foolish.

Peter Wilkie, sitting beside him on a coil of rope, was under no such disadvantage. His feelings were in no wise overpowering, only sufficient to make him wish to be at his best. He had had both measles and calf-love in their appointed season, and in such easy form as his constitution allowed. He had been in love many times, according to his capacity--an easy-going and pleasant acceleration of the pulses, mental and bodily, without fever or foolishness of any kind. The thing ran its course, and went off again as judgment advised, leaving him none the worse, and ready to begin the pretty game again on proper occasion.

Mr Peter considered Margaret a remarkably fine girl--handsome, clever, and with money--who would do him credit as a wife, if he should make up his mind to take her. He had very nearly done so. He would have done so, but that there was another, a competing beauty, as eligible, seemingly, in all respects, and still more attractive. Miss Hillyard was quite as handsome; and if Clam Beach knew less about her fortune, that was the natural consequence of her being from Chicago. Her dress and appointments betokened wealth; and he had gathered from the American boarders that the Deanes, with whom she travelled, were people of note, and very rich. Her complete self-possession showed both that she had lived in the world, and had held a good place in it; and, for herself, she was perhaps handsomer than the other. Their styles were so different that they could not be compared; but if anything, he preferred Miss Hillyard's. Being sandy-haired and pale-eyed himself, the brilliant brunette, with her rich colour, bright eyes, and abundant hair, had the attraction which lies in opposites; and then her conversation and manner were so much more formed and matured than were Margaret's. She was a woman, in fact, while the other was a girl, and, he fancied, would suit him better as a companion.

Miss Hillyard, however, was at the other end of the boat with Mr Naylor, as she so often was now--"Why did she waste so much of her company on that old cod?" he wondered--in the centre of a knot of young people, whose frequent laughter showed that the conversation was general.

Margaret was before him, and glancing up at her where she sat, he doubted if anything could be prettier than the picture she made, under the shadow of her broad-leafed hat, bound with a copious scarf. She had little colour; but the healthy pallor harmonised with the blueness of her violet eyes, and the brown hair escaping into sunshine behind her ear, and flashing like ruddy gold. The colour of her eyes repeated itself in the handkerchief knotted at her throat; and her Holland riding-habit, fitting without a crease, displayed to perfection the lithe young figure, with arms so free and supple. "Cœlebs in search of a wife" began to doubt if this damsel were not the better choice. He coughed to clear his voice, and proceeded to make conversation in his best manner.

He talked about the scenery. The bay reminded him of the Bay of Salerno, and every other bay, seemingly, which he had ever seen in distant places--especially in the Mediterranean--which sounded picturesque and romantic to Margaret, who had never been out of Canada till now, and tended to impress her with his merit as an accomplished traveller and man of the world. He had maundered eastward as far as the Gulf of Corinth, and even alluded casually to the Golden Horn, with the intention of taking it next, waxing eloquent over the glories of Constantinople, and favouring her with recollections and anecdotes of Eastern life, when Petty, standing by disgusted at his exclusion from a conversation in which he could not gain standing-room, cried out--

"See! they are actually launching a big sail-boat up the cove yonder. What can people want with a sail-boat in a calm like this?"

Margaret started and turned round, regardless of the coast of Greece, Dardanelles, and Bosphorus, about which she had been expecting to hear.

"Where are they launching a boat, Mr Petty? Pray show me;" and there came a flush to her cheek, and she looked at him so brightly with a grateful smile, that the young fellow's heart beat faster than before, and he was very happy.

"Do you think they will make out to sail to-day? I wish there would spring up a little wind. Do you not think they will manage to get along, Mr Petty, with skilful steering?"

"I fear, if they do not get under way, they will have little opportunity to steer. When a boat is lying at rest in the water, it does not make any difference how you turn the helm. But see! they are taking out the oars. They will kill themselves in this hot weather. Two men to go rowing a heavy boat like that!"

"Ah, poor fellows! And how they tug and strain to get the great unwieldy thing in motion! They will kill themselves, toiling in the heat--get sunstroke perhaps. How I wish----" but here she stopped short. Perhaps she knew in her heart that she did not wish the thing she had been going to say, or perhaps she thought best to keep her own counsel. She clutched her hands, and wrung them a little, but not enough to be remarkable, and watched the boat.

"What makes her take such interest in the boat?" said Peter within himself. "It sounded as if she wished they had not gone out. But who are they, that she should wish about them? Or perhaps she was wishing that she had not made them go. Ha! that must be it. How eagerly she turned to look when Petty spoke! And who could recognise any one at this distance? Aha! I smell a rat--a lover--a rival. Have a care, Master Peter, or you will miss your footing. Propose and be refused, and look like a fool! Take time, and make sure before you leap."

Walter Petty had heard Margaret's exclamation likewise, but it affected him differently. Either he was too much interested in the young lady, or he was too little interested and hopeful for himself. He had always thought of himself as but a poor creature by the side of Margaret. All that he perceived was, that Margaret took an interest in the boat which he had pointed out, and seemed uneasy about its men working so hard. Why she should be uneasy he did not stop to inquire. It might be the holy pity of her nature, which sympathised with the toils and sufferings of all mankind in a way beyond his ken. It might be anything. He only saw that she was troubled and anxious about that boat and its occupants, and he hastened to mitigate her anxiety.

"It will not be so very hard when they get the boat under way," he said. "Already it goes easier; and see how well they row! They are experienced hands. No; never fear. They will not hurt themselves. And see, out there upon the bay, those moving clouded places! 'Cats'-paws' the sailors call them. They are caused by a puff of air striking the water. When the boatmen get out there, their sail will help them, and I should not wonder but a breeze is springing up, which causes those cats'-paws. Never fear; the boat will do well enough."

He had his reward in the grateful smile with which Margaret regarded him, in looking past his ear at the evolutions of the boat in question, and which made him feel more adult than he had felt in her presence since his lunacy began. The climax of his satisfaction came when she began to speak--

"How much you know about sailing and the sea, Mr Petty! and how interesting it is, to be sure! Yes, really; I must watch that boat to see it work into the breezy water. But of course; there is breeze even here. See how my handkerchief flutters when I hold it out;" and it seemed to Peter Wilkie, looking on, that one of the boatmen thereupon drew out a handkerchief and wiped his forehead.

"Hm," he muttered below his breath. "Look out, Peter Wilkie!"

Walter Petty explained to Margaret that the breeze which stirred her handkerchief arose not from the motion of the air, but from their own motion through it.

"You seem to know everything, Mr Petty, about boats and sailing; and I am so ignorant. Tell me all you know. It seems so mysterious that--that pressing the tiller, for instance, to one side should make the boat go to the other;" and Margaret turned round full front to Petty--it *may* have been past his ear that she was looking--with her profile towards Wilkie, whose countenance fell a little as he asked himself--

"Does she guess that I have been smelling out her little game?"

The "smelling out" had seemed droll to him the moment before; but now, when this slight sign of displeasure--if it were a sign--might be taken as confirmation, it was not so amusing. And yet the girl seemed a finer girl than ever, now that he suspected a rival, and perhaps a favoured rival, in her regard. He was not going to be allowed to play sultan, it appeared, throwing his handkerchief as he pleased, without fear of refusal; wherefore he ceased to question the value of the prize, and began really to think that he desired it.

What would Mrs Naylor, sitting complacently within touch of her daughter, and accepting the conversation of her friends, have said, had she known the suspicion which had crossed the mind of Peter? Margaret was safe at her elbow, and receiving the attentions of the two most eligible young men on board. She would not have believed that her girl, open as the day, truehearted and candid to a fault, could be signalling to a man--a man unrecognisable for the distance--out there in an open boat on Lippenstock Bay. A proceeding on her part so bold and so underhand was impossible. And yet, if it were true, whose fault was it but her own? Oppression, it has been said, will drive a wise man mad. And this was only a girl, pushed, by nagging and injudicious curbing, after a course of equally imprudent liberty, to take her own way. She had but herself to thank, whatever might happen.

Mothers can remember their children as babies; they have tended and ruled them through the years of growth with undisputed sway, and maturity arrives so imperceptibly that it is natural they should not perceive when the term of their reign has come--that the sceptre has withered like a reed, and the children have grown to be women, with wills and rights and aspirations of their own.

CHAPTER XVII.

FESSENDEN'S ISLAND.

The steamer throbbed and snorted on its voyage round the bay, like some big amphibian of palæozoic times, parting the glassy waters right and left, and leaving a long regurgitating trail of swelling waves and eddies in its wake. The sun, now overhead, shed down his beams with an unmitigated ardour, and the water cast back the glare with blistering intensity. There really had arisen a languid air-current from the shore, as Walter Petty had predicted; but the boat was now heading down the bay towards the open sea, and travelling with the breeze, so that on board it seemed to have fallen calm, and was hot and stifling to a degree.

The chat among the voyagers flickered low, and then went out, like the flame of candles in an unwholesome well. Every one sought for shade, and gasped beneath an umbrella, or in some darkened corner of the saloon, collapsed and listless. But the steamer snorted on its way, regardless of their comfort, and gleeful, as it seemed, in the increasing heat; for now she belched forth smoke, and weltered in it, letting it curl and twist about her fore and aft, borne on the chasing breeze--as though the sportive monster were shaking out her mane, as is said to be the wont of the sea-serpent when he rises from the deep to fright lone mariners. She had grown fiendish in her mood, that misguided steamer, filling the air with foulness, and showering smuts on the white umbrellas, the fresh toilets, and even the dainty nose of beauty. It grew intolerable, and the passengers might have risen in mutiny and altered the vessel's course, but that the heat had left them limp and lacking energy. They only groaned and imprecated; while the steersman stood like a wooden image by the wheel, one turn of which would have blown away the mischief, looking at their misery with unwinking eyes, and laughing mayhap down deep within his wooden ribs.

The mouth of the bay was reached in time, and the islands with their straits and narrows, and winding channels running in between; and beyond, the blue Atlantic. A new life breathed on them the moment they passed the cape which terminates the bay. Like pent-up invalids escaping from a sickroom, they held up their faces to the sky to drink great breaths of freshness. Out there it is always cool, however the sun may beat. They threaded the channels among the islands, and then sailed out into the far-extending blue, and were refreshed.

Noon was long passed, although they had breakfasted early, before it occurred to any one to feel hungry; but at length the idea of luncheon presented itself to many minds about the same time, as something which would be agreeable. The steamer was put about, and they returned back among the islands. One of them, Fessenden's Island by name, lay most open to the ocean, and farther out than the others. On this they landed. It seemed intended by nature for their purpose, having a little cove with shelving bottom which admitted their vessel, and a seaward boundary of rocky ledges sinking perpendicularly in deep water on the inward side, so that they could moor themselves to the shore as comfortably as at a wharf, without the inconvenient intervention of the boats.

The hotel servants quickly got their hampers landed, and soon the repast was spread in the slowly broadening shadow of neighbouring rocks, while the party encamped beneath their umbrellas on the scrubby sea-grass, or fetched themselves seats from the ship hard by. The clatter of knives and plates, the popping of corks, and the din of voices, startled the sea-fowl where they perched overhead; they screeched and fluttered angrily at the unwonted disturbance, and taking to the wing, they wheeled and circled in the air above, surveying the intruders, and eyeing the meats which fear alone prevented their pouncing down on and bearing away, and finally, with a parting scream, flew seaward in a long white trail and disappeared.

The tide had turned. Two hours were allowed to spend on shore. After that, the steamer was to blow its whistle, and they must re-embark and get away, or the ship would be left stranded by the ebb, to await the following tide. The party having refreshed, broke up, and wandered apart as chance directed, to explore the island. Mrs Naylor found herself comfortable in her chair. Uneven walking over rocks presented no attractions. Digestion and fresh air, combined with snatches of light reading and chit-chat, seemed a more rational enjoyment. "But, Margaret, my dear, I will not interfere with your more energetic tastes," she said; "you can go, if you like, and scramble on the rocks like the rest. I shall do nicely with these ladies. Mr Wilkie, I am sure, will kindly see that you do not fall over a precipice."

Mr Wilkie rose alertly, and Margaret followed. She had meant to go away more quietly, later on, under the care of Walter Petty, whom she noticed lingering within call. He was so devotedly kind and respectful, that the girl could not but have a kindness for him. He would have liked to go, she saw, and he would have answered better for the purpose she had in view; though it was not, as he might fondly hope, to purr soft nothings in sequestered nooks. However, fate and her mother had imposed the more self-satisfied and confident gallant, and she must submit; though she felt a qualm of self-reproach in meeting the other's glance, in which disappointment seemed blended with a shade of remonstrance. Had she not shown a preference for him in the boat over that long-tongued rival, whom he cordially detested?--turned away from his longwinded rigmarole about travel, to ask sensible information from himself? There was no understanding those girls, and no use trusting them. And yet this one was so--so--what was she not, in fact? But it was desolating, all the same. He could not bring himself to join any one else, though there were "fellows" as well as girls who would have been glad of his company. There was his pipe, however, that silent friend, so soothing and so unobtrusive in its consolations. He would have recourse to that; and scrambling out to the extremity of the ledge beyond the steamboat, he sat him down beside the sad sea wave and blew a melancholy cloud.

Margaret and Wilkie scrambled along the shore, made difficult with rocks and heaped-up boulders. They clambered briskly enough until they had doubled a promontory which secluded them from observation, and then Mr Peter heaved a sigh of mingled relief and exhaustion.

"What an abominable way we have come, Miss Naylor! I am fairly blown. Here is a smooth rock at last; let us sit and enjoy the view."

"I am not tired at all, Mr Wilkie. Let us get on."

"I do not think we can, Miss Margaret. The shore grows steeper. We should have to take to those rocks lower down, all wet and slimy. It is scarcely safe. Look at the view from here! Look at the expanse of sea! It might be the Mediterranean, so blue and sunny. And those banks of cloud along the horizon--are they not fine?"

"Very fine, Mr Wilkie, but I want to see the island."

"My dear young lady, islands are all the same, and one part of one of them is just like another part. We need not flounder farther than we have come already, to know this one by heart. It is ditto all over--rocks sticking out of the water to support a little earth and a few sea-birds."

"But I have never been upon an island before, except those wooded ones on the St Lawrence, which do not at all answer to your description. They are nests floating on the water, and simply lovely. I want to see more of this one. Our St Lawrence islands are covered with trees. Are there none here?"

"Too exposed here, you may be sure. A gooseberry-bush would be blown down in the winter gales, not to speak of a tree. Besides, we really cannot go farther along this detestable shore. The sharp stones will cut the boot-soles off your feet."

"Then let us go inland. Why should we keep to the shore? The ground slopes up easily enough; let us go to the top and gain a bird's-eye view of the island. No, really, I could not think of sitting down. We shall have more than enough of that in the steamboat before we get home."

And so the young man, finding he could not persuade, had perforce to let himself be persuaded, and follow when he would have led--or rather, sat down.

The slope was not very steep, though it was longer than Peter would have expected a walk on so small an island could be; but at length they reached the rounded flatness of the summit, and looked around. The island spread out beneath on every side, and the sister islands were marshalled north and south like sentinels to guard the inner waters. Lippenstock Bay lay within them, a burnished glass throwing back the sunshine; and the country beyond looked higher, more varied and important than when seen from the water-level. An unmistakable breeze had now sprung up, and was carrying straggling wreaths of cloud before it, the vanguard of more solid masses which were creeping up the sky from the distant west. Eastward the ocean now had lost its sapphire blueness and grown dull and grey, while far out toward the horizon it lowered beneath the oncome of the rising clouds, great cumulus masses lifting themselves in heaven and advancing against the breeze. They caught the rays of the opposing sun upon their breasts, and flashed them back, and sprinkled them on the sea, turning its lively blue to a white sickly grey.

"What splendid clouds!" cried Margaret. "But there will be a storm. When those clouds from the east meet the clouds in the west, we shall have thunder."

"I remember a sky the day I crossed the St Gothard, going down into the plains of Italy. Very fine it was----"

"Yes; I daresay it would be. The Old World must be a very superior place to this poor continent of ours. Even the sun and moon must shine better over there, by all accounts. The wonder is, how any of you travelled folks ever cared to come here at all. But say! there is quite a breeze coming down the bay; where can that sail-boat we were watching have gone? I cannot make out a sail anywhere. Is it the dazzle from the water that conceals it, do you think? Or can it be hid behind one of the islands, I wonder?"

"I see something white flapping behind that promontory down there, where the channel narrows between this island and the next. There it falls! They have taken it down. The men must be landing."

"Where? Ah! let us run down and see."

Peter would have liked to bite his tongue. Found guilty of that offence unpardonable in trans-Atlantic eyes, of praising the Old World at the expense of the New, he had thought to make his peace by discovering for his companion the object for which her eyes were searching the prospect; and he had done it with a vengeance. Not only was the offence forgotten, but himself seemed likely to be forgotten or overlooked as well. To think that he could be *gauche* enough to conduct his fair one into the arms of the very rival who had aroused his suspicion that morning! He had forgotten since then; things had gone so smoothly and pleasantly. What an awakening! "Duffer!" he muttered below his breath, and felt humbled indeed. But he made one poor struggle with destiny ere he yielded. He pulled out his watch, and asked his companion with a start if she had any idea what was the hour.

"The tide is turning, you must remember," he added. "We shall hear the whistle within fifteen minutes, and the steamer cannot wait. The skipper says she will be grounded by the ebb if we are not off by four. And a storm is coming on. I declare I hear distant thunder already. How dim the light is getting, too! It will take all we can do to be back in time. We have only twenty minutes."

"Your watch must be fast," and Margaret pulled out her own. "Ten minutes past three I make it, and I know mine is fast. See the groups scattered all over the island! No one has thought of turning yet. There is Judge Petty with his hammer pounding specimens out of yon cliff. Yonder is my sister with somebody picking flowers for her. Nobody thinks of gathering *me* a bouquet, ever. There is a party down there in the hollow, and I can distinguish Lettice Deane's voice quite plainly; and far over are two people standing on the edge of a cliff showing like silhouettes against the open sea. Uncle Joseph is one of them. No one is thinking of turning back."

"But, Miss Naylor, the storm will be on directly. Observe how dim it grows. You will get drenched with rain."

"I don't think it will rain till evening."

"Indeed it will. See how the clouds are coming up! Hear to the rumbling thunder!"

"I am not afraid. But if you think otherwise, I should not like to spoil your pleasure with the prospect of a wetting. Good-bye. You can tell them to expect me shortly." And she skipped away.

There was nothing for Peter but to follow, little as he could expect his presence to be welcome when they should come on that rival at the bottom of the hill. He hated the fellow, of course, and wished him "far enough," but he could not help feeling curious to see him. Yet he followed without alacrity. For the sake of argument, he had spoken of the light as growing dim; now he felt it to be so indeed. The warmth and brightness had gone out of the day for him, and it was become a common thing. Not that he would have said so. The poet's trick of drawing voices from inanimate nature to express or sympathise with his momentary emotions was none of his. He was matter-of-fact and common-sensical to a degree, if at the same time lucid-minded and intelligent: but still he was human like the rest of us; and for that matter so is the poet, "fed with the same food, hurt with the same weapons, subject to the same diseases." If he were not, what would his utterances be worth? His gift is utterance, but the thing he utters must be within the possibility of all to feel. And Peter felt, though the influence had stolen on him unawares. He had been in Margaret's company through successive hours, and she was a flower too fresh and sweet for any insect to have fluttered round so long without becoming intoxicated somewhat with the fragrance.

At the bottom of the hill, behind an intervening rock, they came upon a sandy beach, the extremity of a bar which runs across to the nearest island, connecting the two at low water, and forming the only landing-place other than that of which the steamer had possession. The boatmen were securing their craft as the two came in view. One of them with a shout sprang forward and bounded up the steep to meet them. He seized both Margaret's hands and shook them rapturously; then, remembering that she had a companion, to be accepted as a necessary evil, he turned round to Peter, raised his hat, and ceremoniously wished him good-day.

Peter returned the salute, and looked curiously in the other's face to divine what manner of man this favoured one might be, if haply he might yet be dealt with, outmanœuvred, or supplanted, and recognised with astonishment that it was "that" young Blount who had spent a few days at Clam Beach. His feelings expressed themselves in a low, scarce audible whistle; and circumstances, looks, tones, details from the week before, so trivial that he had not been conscious of remembering them, sprang suddenly into knowledge and arranged themselves; as when a thread is dropped into a chemical solution, crystals gather from the fluid, and shape themselves with mathematical precision round the nucleus. The circumstances strung themselves in an induction amounting to demonstration, that Margaret Naylor had bestowed her regards, and that he had come too late into the field.

The young people were assiduously polite to Mr Peter. They did not wish that unkind rumours of their meeting should circulate in the hotel, and they would not request him to keep a secret for them--their feelings would not permit them to do that--so both endeavoured to conciliate his goodwill. They did what they could to include him in their conversation; but he was inattentive, answering at random or not at all. The sudden revelation had confused him like a blow, and his thoughts kept wandering back to the details on which his induction was based, trying them and endeavouring to shake their consistency, wondering that he had not read the truth before, and pitying himself in what now seemed his disappointment.

His answers were made at random, but they did not observe it. They were feeding their eyes upon each other's faces, after a three days' separation, and they had no thought for anything but the delight of being together. How good it was! They babbled, scarcely knowing what they spoke of, and any observation which Peter chose to interject was perfectly good as conversation in their eyes, sitting there together on the shore, touching one another, looking shyly in each other's eyes, hearing each other's voices, and being happy. Peter lounged beside them on the ground, twisting his awkward limbs into uncouth knots, and feeling dull and flattened out, defeated and humbled, though nobody had done anything to him whatever.

And time and tide went on their wonted course, but no one of the three took notice of their passing.

CHAPTER XVIII.

AN ADIEU.

The cloud-masses in the east had risen over half the sky. They now presented only a rim of flashing white along the upper edge towards the sun. The concave vault within was dim and lowering, and was advancing visibly upon the darkened sea. Low sighing voices came across the water, with the continuous flickering of far-off lightning and the grumble of distant thunder. The sea was no longer asleep, as it had been an hour ago beneath the placid light. A rolling glassy swell, which momentarily grew heavier and higher, was coming in from the ocean. The steamer at its mooring no longer lay firm and still like part of the adjacent rocks. It rose and fell obedient to the undulations, and strained upon its cables. The tide was ebbing. Not many inches now interposed between the bottom and its keel; and as the swell grew higher, there was danger that ere long she would bump upon the rocks.

The captain, watch in hand, grew restless and impatient. The passengers' time ashore was hardly yet run out, but every minute had grown precious, and he longed to be afloat. He tugged the whistle-chain, and startled the still air with loud discordant yells, then ran, gesticulating and shouting, to the poop, to warn those at hand that they must hurry on board, as there was no time to lose. The loungers rose and stretched themselves, unwilling to be disturbed; but there was something imperious in the short shrill screeches of the whistle, and they obeyed. The strollers heard and turned, and even ran when they came in sight and saw the excited skipper swinging his arms, and the men already preparing to cast loose from the shore.

In a wonderfully short space the deck was alive with passengers and the shore deserted. The skipper cast a searching look along the higher grounds within sight. There was no sign of human presence remaining on the island. The whistle uttered a last long melancholy scream of parting, and was silent, the steamer lurched upon the swell, and they were out in deep water.

The passengers separated into groups and rested, like the sediment of troubled water in a pool, watching the oncoming of the storm, as to which there could now be no mistake. Already the first eddies of the rising wind were coming from the east, and the sea was rising rapidly, making landsmen feel sedate in anticipation of that worst evil of the deep, the qualms of sickness.

There was one, however, on whom the heavings had no effect. Her mind was disturbed; bodily discomfort was forgot, or only added to her anxiety.

She got up from her seat and reeled across the deck to Mrs Naylor, who sat buried in pathetic silence, awaiting whatever might be in store.

"Mrs Naylor, what ever has come of my Peter?" she said. "I cannot see him anywhere. He always comes to look after his old mother. Where is he now?"

"I do not know, Mrs Wilkie. This motion is dreadful. Oh, how could I be so foolish as venture out to sea on this horrid little boat!"

"But you *must* know, Mrs Naylor; I saw that girl of yours taking him away, and I have not seen sight of him since. What has she done with him? Oh, those girls! they will be the death of me."

"He certainly took Margaret for a walk, but I have not seen them since. No doubt they are in the cabin lying down. I wish I were there. I wish I were anywhere rather than here. This see-saw motion is dreadful."

"What a woman! And she calls herself a mother! I wonder ye don't think shame, ma'am, sitting there at your ease, and never minding what comes of your own daughter. But she's foisted her on my poor Peter, and that's all she cares for. And she's not minding what I say wan bit. Oh, thae Canadian women!"

Mrs Naylor was too poorly to rejoin. Engrossed in her own misery, she probably did not hear.

"Here you! Steward, waiter, whatever ye are," cried Mrs Wilkie, "go down to the cabin. I would break my neck if I ventured through this feckless crowd. See if ye can find Mr Wilkie--a big handsome gentleman. Ye can't mistake him. Tell him his mother's up here, and wants him."

The messenger went, and returned, and was sent over all the ship, in vain. The missing man was neither to be found nor heard of, and it was discovered that Margaret Naylor was missing likewise.

"Oh, captain, captain! put back--put back! You've left Mr Wilkie behind."

"Impossible, ma'am. We couldn't get in at the landing now. The weather is growing worse, and we must make what speed we can back into the bay. This is not a sea-going craft."

"But you've left my boay on a desert island, and ye'll have murder or marrich on your soul. Ye *must* go back; or I'll have the law of ye as soon as ever I get my fut on dry land."

"We might never reach dry land at all, if we were to put back in the weather that is coming on. The gentleman is quite safe. The fishermen have a cabin, round the island at the other landing. He'll be all right, and comfortable."

"Why will ye not go to the other landing, and see? to ease a mother's feelin's."

"There's a sand-bar there. We could not get near the shore."

"Ye might try. Ye could send your boat for them.... Yonder! I see a black thing moving.... He'll be dead or married before morning. Oh, captain!... Turn!... For pity's sake!"

The captain turned and looked in the old woman's face, whose eyes, already full, were on the point of brimming over. The alternative she named seemed rather an anticlimax, and not so very harrowing. He would have liked, himself, to be offered such a choice, but fate had never so favoured him.

"He'll do, ma'am. She ain't half bad, the craft he has in tow. She's right and tight. I saw them steering off together."

"He'll be done for, ye scoffin' reprobate! Ye think it fine fun, I daresay; but it's no joke to a man in his poseetion. The girl's well enough, for anything I know. In fack, I thought her not amiss. But marryin's an expurriment ye can try but wance; and I want to make sure before I give my leave.... Do you no see yon black thing movin', captain? It's him! I'm sure of it. Turn!... like a lamb!" and she held out her hands.

The lamb smiled within his beard; but the blandishment was unavailing. "There's nothing moving but the ship, ma'am; and she'll have to move faster, or worse will happen;" and so saying, he escaped to the engine-room to crack on more steam.

Mrs Wilkie was in despair. She clasped her hands and staggered to the taffrail, to gaze her last and fondest on the retreating island. She clung to the flagstaff, with eyes streaming tears, and her short grey curls draggling in the wind. She even waved her parasol in sad adieu; but the wind, ere long, caught hold of that, and spread it out, and twitched it from her grasp, and sent it spinning through the air away to leeward. Anon she waved her handkerchief, when she could spare it from its duty at her eyes, clinging to her flagstaff, swaying and swinging, heaving and falling, with the motion of the vessel, till the pitiless ocean asserted its cruel rights, and she sank a sea-sick Niobe upon the deck.

CHAPTER XIX.

STORM-STAYED.

His niece's eyesight was not at fault when she thought that she recognised Joseph Naylor's figure silhouetted against the horizon. It was he indeed, and he was not alone. That was the sweetest walk, he told himself, which he had ever taken. It was the happiest day; and he looked back in his tranquil bliss, standing with eyes which rested dreamily upon the sea; and, forgetting to converse, he wondered if the unreasoning transports he had known in youth were to be compared to this.

It seemed like the warm radiance of an unclouded afternoon succeeding a day of rain which has been ushered in by deceitful sun-bursts, sent, as it were, to deepen the succeeding gloom. The peace and trust, and the contented sense of basking, without a wish left unfulfilled, were inexpressibly sweet. The sense of doubleness, which had disturbed his earlier intercourse with his companion, had disappeared. His spiritual eyes had focussed themselves into agreement, and now the two images were blended into one. It was the first and only tenderness of his life, stifled though still smouldering beneath the years of widowhood, on which this stranger had chanced to let in air; and the spark divine had awoke among its ashes, and was again aflame.

Words he had none just then. His being was strung too high for the vibrations to be made audible in common utterance. He was only receptive now, drinking in influence from her presence, but making no response. They had been together all the day. In the morning they had been gay at the cheerful starting. They had been conversational as the day waxed warmer, companionable when it threatened to grow oppressive, and they had felt like very old friends who understood each other thoroughly, when they set out to walk.

The extreme tranquillity at which they had now arrived was a little more complete than Rose Hillyard altogether enjoyed. Fortunately she was sympathetic by nature, and understood a great deal more than was conveyed to her by words. She appreciated the silence--felt, indeed, that it was the highest compliment, or rather something immeasurably beyond compliment; but ere long she began to wish that it would not last much longer.

The mind of Rose was not altogether so utterly at ease as it appeared, though she would not for the world that any one should have so suspected. She would have done violence to herself, even, sooner than acknowledge in her heart that she was not at peace; but still there was a fever in her blood, making her restless, and eager to be doing, and drown an inarticulate yearning for something she would not name.

The silence drove her back upon herself, and gave voices opportunity to make themselves audible within--voices she had endeavoured to silence, and forbidden to be there. "If the man would only say something! If he would even flirt!" That was a pretty game which she believed she understood and could play with the best. But this was not flirtation: it was right down solemn earnest; and she was pleased in thinking that it was. A good man's happiness was in her hands; and more, she liked the man, and believed, I dare affirm--though we must not say "intended to accept" what has not yet been offered--that when he declared himself she would lend a friendly ear.

And yet she had rather he would have flirted. The stir and interest of the game would have afforded the excitement for which she craved. It was but a game, and could be played without a second thought. The serious thing was different. So much depends on it, that people play it slower; and they play it with the heart, and not the head, which is the more nimble member. It was movement and excitement for which her fibres ached; though peace, if that had been attainable, had been far more precious.

"How fond you must be of the sea!" she said at last. "We seem to have been standing here a long time."

Joseph started, and turned. Her voice had broken in upon a reverie which could not be called a day-dream. It had been too passive for succession of ideas, and was rather a receptive bathing in the blissfulness of the situation. But yet no waking could have been sweeter than the sound of that voice which now addressed him. It was the same which he remembered long ago, whose echoes had thrilled him in his dreams, and made his wakings sorrowful to find it was not there. It was with a smile and a deep full breath of satisfaction that he turned to his companion.

"Forgive me," he said. "It is so pleasant being here, that I forgot about passing time.... Yes, I am fond of the sea. I always was. I left home to go to sea when I was a boy--could not stay away from it. It is so big and so even, and it changes under one's very eye, you can't tell how. It feels as if it were alive--a being that could understand your thoughts without your telling them."

"So it does. I know the feeling, although I never attempted to put it into words.... The sea is company--when one is alone; but now----?" and she looked up in his eyes with the flicker of a smile which was scarcely reproachful, yet not quite humorous.

"Most true," he answered, smiling in reply. "The silent communion with Nature is not a sociable observance; and, as you say, we must have stood here a good while. Let's follow this footpath. It seems to run round the island on the inner side. The walking will be easier, and we shall get back sooner than by crossing the hill as we came."

The path ran for a time along the edge of cliffs, which stood some forty or fifty feet above the sea, and sank sheer down into deep water, fretting the smooth green billows rolling by into a fringe of foam. Turning with the rounding of the land, the path struck down upon the leeward side of the island and ran along the shore.

"Should we not hurry?" Rose Hillyard observed. "The tide must have sunk a long way since we left the steamer. See those rocks covered with wet seaweed. They must have been under water this last tide, and now they are feet above it. The captain spoke about the tide, and his fear of stranding, and being forced to wait twelve hours for next high water. Must we not make haste?"

"I do not see why we should disturb ourselves. There are three of our people yonder, sitting on a sandhill and at ease. Had we not better do likewise? They seem happy.... As for me, I have no watch, and no care for time. Let us be guided by *them*."

"And my watch has stopped, or something. Well!... I hope those others are keeping track of the time.... Yes, it is nice here. The air is more still than it was on the cliffs, and yet not so hot. But is the light not growing dim? This is pleasanter than the glare of mid-day. Why can it not be always afternoon? Yet, has it not come on us rather suddenly?"

They were sitting now, and their talk was dribbling along in an easy, drowsy way, such as might be expected from people who had been for so many hours in each other's company. It was after luncheon, after a walk, after a day whose heat and blazing brightness had only been made tolerable by fresh sea-air, in itself a form of stimulation. Their nerves, all day kept tense, were relaxing now, and a restful feeling, born of harmonious companionship, was extending from the mind into the physical system, and producing a tranquillity in which content was verging towards lethargy. In fact, they were a little tired, and more than a little sleepy. Head propped on hand, and that supported on the extended elbow, they reclined upon the bent which clothed a swelling sandhill. Conversation grew intermittent and monosyllabic, and then ceased--their eyelids growing momentarily heavier without their being aware.

A shrill reverberation broke upon the air. It stopped, and began anew, and ended in a volley of shrill, short, barking shrieks. Joseph lifted his head and looked about. He had forgot about the steamboat, and the idea of its whistling a recall did not occur to him It was sea-fowl he thought of in that solitary place, and he wondered drowsily at the harshness of their cry, and their strength of lung. He threw a listless glance aloft, but not a wing was visible over all the sky; only the sun was veiled now in a cloud, and did not dazzle--which was comfortable, and made the restful feeling more complete.

The next sensation he was conscious of was damp. Big drops of rain were lighting on his face, and wetting his limbs through the thin summer clothing. He started now. Yes, he must have slept. The sky was black, and the scene grown dim like twilight. Like twilight for an instant, and then a blinding flash made everything intensely visible, and the heavens seemed to crack above the trembling earth with loud reverberating thunder.

He started and laid his hand on his companion's shoulder.

"Rosa!"--How sweet the name felt on his lips, even in his hurry! It was his first time to use it. But had he the right?--"Miss Hillyard! Arouse! A storm is coming on. You will be drenched. Arouse!"

Rose opened her eyes. She looked straight in his, and with a pleasant smile. It was an instant before she was fully conscious of the situation--so sweet an instant! Then she was herself, and sprang to her feet.

"We must run! But where? How wrong of me to sleep!" It was Joseph who spoke. "Ha! down yonder on the beach I see a boat. We may find shelter for you near there."

The lightning flashed incessantly. The air quivered with the resounding thunderclaps succeeding one another without interval or pause. The rain streamed down. The windows of heaven were opened, and the waters of the firmament descended in sheets, as if to overwhelm the earth.

He took her hand, and they hurried along the sands towards the boat, as quickly as they could, by the gleam of the intermittent flashes, which blinded while they lasted, and yet made the intervals between seem dark as night by contrast.

A halloo reached them as they stumbled on, and made them turn aside, where, in a sheltered corner, stood the fishermen's hut. They were inside in a moment, still dazed and panting from the buffeting storm, and streaming with rain, though the time they had been exposed to it was shorter than it has taken to relate. Grateful for the shelter, they recognised that it was Blount and Wilkie who had hailed them, while Margaret stood within, coaxing some dying embers into flame with the aid of a fan and some fresh fuel, preparatory to drying herself; for she too had been caught in the rain, though she had not been drenched as Rose was. The men, watching the storm from the open door, had seen the others hurrying by, and had hailed them to the shelter they would otherwise have missed.

"You?" cried Walter Blount, in a tone which betrayed perhaps a shade of disappointment as well as the natural surprise. He had known of the expedition to Fessenden's Island, and had sailed thither in hopes of what would scarcely be an accidental meeting, and he had been fortunate beyond his expectation. When the whistle of the steamer had sounded, he had heard, but Margaret had taken no heed, and Wilkie in his discomfiture, had seemingly not observed. It would have been gratuitous on his part, he thought, to disturb the harmony and precipitate a parting, seeing that he had a boat of his own, in which they could return at any time. If Wilkie would have gone, it would have been better still, only that Margaret must have accompanied him; wherefore he exerted himself to brighten the talk, and keep their thoughts as far as possible from the subject of the steamer; and to his own surprise he succeeded, for he could not understand why "*that fellow Wilkie*" should feel engrossed.

And perhaps the "fellow" was not, but only mortified and squelched at the unwonted neglect into which he, who had come to look on himself as an invincible lady-killer, had fallen. Anything seemed better to him than the shame of returning to the steamer alone. How would he feel when asked what he had done with his companion? And, foolishly, he had a misgiving that if he proposed to return, she would not accompany him. Her attention was now transferred entirely to the rival, and he found himself nowhere. But he would stick to her like a burr. One can sometimes spoil a game which one cannot join in. He was sure the rival wished him away; and that was reason enough for sticking fast and showing no sign. By-and-by, when the other was gone, the lady would be more amenable to his displeasure, and then would be his time to show it.

As time wore on, the sky grew dark, and presently the storm was upon them. They retreated to the hut, and then Margaret remembered about the steamboat. Wilkie looked at his watch, and said they had outstayed their time; but the deluge of rain made it impossible now to set out on the return. Blount's man was despatched to warn the skipper, and they resigned themselves to await the subsidence of the storm. The last users of the hut had left a fire behind them, of which a coal or two still smouldered in the ashes; and Margaret, uneasy at the account she should have to render by-and-by, made busy in rekindling the blaze, rather than resign herself to forebodings of a maternal lecture.

"You?" was Blount's exclamation, repeated a second time, when the newcomers entered the hut; and the tone of disappointment verged closely on disgust. Joseph Naylor was his friend, but at that moment he would have preferred almost any other intruder. He was his friend, but he was also Margaret's uncle, and therefore the most unwelcome man who could have appeared. Standing by the open door and listening to the thunder and the falling rain, after despatching his boatman to the steamer, he had been building himself a castle in the air. The steamboat would be gone when his messenger reached the landing. The man, while obeying, had assured him of that, as it was only at the height of the tide that she was able to approach the island. The steamboat being gone, Margaret must take passage back with him in his sail-boat. Landed at Lippenstock together, it would not be hard to give Wilkie the slip; and then, behind a lively trotter, they could start for parts unknown. It would be days before the family could overtake them. Ere then they would be man and wife, and the family would gladly make the best of what it could no longer prevent. He had never known Margaret so soft and sweetly amenable to influence as she had been these last two hours. Fortune seemed to have softened her mood on purpose to assist him. He felt sure he could persuade her; and here, at the very turning-point of his fate, appeared uncle Joseph, "*a god out of a machine*," to spoil all. It was unspeakably grievous.

Wilkie cried "You!" at the same moment as Walter; but the tone was different. There was hope and relief in both his face and voice, in marked contrast with the other. Consolation, hope, indemnity for slights, all shone before his view in the appearance of Rose Hillyard. She was escorted, to be sure, but only by "old Naylor"--a man half as old again as himself, and not nearly so polished or agreeable. "The Hillyard" had often struck him as in many respects superior to Margaret Naylor. At the worst, to form one in a quintet could not but be pleasanter than he had found the part of supernumerary in a trio. He positively beamed upon the newcomers, and would willingly have heaped wood on the fire, and even assisted Rose to make herself comfortable; but she assured him that Margaret Naylor and herself could do everything, and he must rejoin the men in the porch without, or, like Peeping Tom of Coventry, he might find himself struck blind on the spot.

END OF THE FIRST VOLUME.

Milton Keynes UK
Ingram Content Group UK Ltd.
UKHW031631231024
450082UK00005B/431